LITERATURE OF MYSTICISM IN WESTERN TRADITION

By the same author

By the same author

THE TRANSFORMATION OF SIN:
Studies in Donne, Herbert, Vaughan and Traherne

IMAGES AND IDEAS IN LITERATURE OF THE
ENGLISH RENAISSANCE

SIX MODERN AUTHORS AND PROBLEMS OF BELIEF

LITERATURE OF MYSTICISM IN WESTERN TRADITION

Patrick Grant

St. Martin's Press   New York

ISBN 0–312–48808–4

Library of Congress Cataloging in Publication Data

Grant, Patrick.
  Literature of mysticism in Western tradition.

  Bibliography: p.
  1. Mysticism—Addresses, essays, lectures.   I. Title.
BV5082.2.G72   1982   248.2′2   82–5789
ISBN 0–312–48808–4   AACR2

In memory of
O. P. Melvin

'Oh Lov what hast Thou don!'
Thomas Traherne

Contents

Preface

A central claim of these essays is that mysticism cannot be well discussed separately from a framework of faith. Consequently, I speak about some aspects of literature of mysticism in the Latin West because the culture and language which most fully claim one's allegiance – in which, so to speak, one has most faith – provide the best means for coming to terms with a subject which suggests that without faith is no understanding.

I concentrate on literature in order to maintain that if one is to describe the mystical fact in words, the combination of passionate conviction, discrimination and insight which characterises great poetry and the critic's reaction to it, is the most adequate means for grasping the essentially analogous relationship between spiritual experience and tradition. The manner in which mysticism is, in this sense, a kind of poetry of religion is best understood by looking at the writings of those who are first mystics and then authors, rather than at the work of poets who write on mystical subjects, but who may or may not be mystics. Of course, this priority cannot be rigorously maintained, but it is a tendency of the ensuing discussion.

I was prompted to write on mysticism because my earlier books led me naturally to it, and because the present state of discussion on the subject called for comment from the point of view of literary criticism. In the influential *Sacramentum Mundi*, the theologian Heribert Fischer writes that 'critical hermeneutics is urgently required; especially for all types of "literary" mysticism', and strong recent contributions by philosophers (for instance Katz (ed.), *Mysticism and Philosophical Analysis*), and researchers in comparative religion (for instance Staal, *Exploring Mysticism. A Methodological Essay*) make Fischer's observation all the more pertinent. I therefore found it inviting to attempt some response, in however small a way.

At the end of each chapter is a selection of texts which are relevant to matters raised in the argument, and which seem to be striking in their own right, or part of a coherent literary expression of the life of contemplative prayer. The end notes are intended to document the discussion and to provide a guide for further reading.

I thank Charles Doyle, René Hague, Laurence Lerner, Jim Mackey and Tony Nuttall, who read the typescript and made numerous valuable suggestions. A Leave Fellowship from the Social Sciences and Humanities Research Council of Canada made possible the completion of the typescript, and permissions have been granted by the following: the Iona Community for permission to reprint selections from *Mechthild of Magdeburg, The Revelations of Mechthild of Magdeburg (1210–97), or The Flowing Light of the Godhead*, trans. Lucy Menzies; the Longman Group Ltd for permission to reprint selections from Evelyn Underhill, *The Letters*, ed. Charles Williams; the Putnam Publishing Group and Routledge and Kegan Paul Ltd for permission to reprint selections from Simone Weil, *Waiting for God*, trans. Emma Crauford; William B. Eerdmans Publishing Company and David Higham Associates Ltd for permission to reprint selections from Charles Williams, *Descent of the Dove*; The Franciscan Herald Press for permission to reprint selections from *The Works of Bonaventure*, trans. José de Vinck; Cistercian Publications for permission to reprint selections from William of St Thierry, *The Enigma of Faith*, and Evagrius Ponticus, *Praktikos and Chapters on Prayer*, copyright Cistercian Publications, Kalamazoo, Michigan. Selections from *Mystical Writings of Rulman Merswin*, edited and interpreted by Thomas S. Kepler, © W.L. Jenkins MCMLX, are used by permission of The Westminster Press. Selections from Thomas Merton, *New Seeds of Contemplation*, copyright © 1961 by the Abbey of Gethsemani, Inc., are reprinted by permission of New Directions Publishing Corporation, and Anthony Clarke Books. Selections from Richard of St Victor are reprinted by permission of Faber and Faber Ltd from *Richard of Saint Victor: Selected Writings on Contemplation*.

P.G.

CHAPTER ONE
Mysticism, Faith and Culture

Solitude is not isolation. The latter is savage; the former a mode of access to mystery, enhancing life with subtlety of feeling, compassion and understanding. A person deprived of solitude becomes a cog in a machine, unaware of his own inner life or the inner lives of others. Yet solitude sought merely as a refuge from the general human condition courts misanthropy: a person is neither wholly unique nor wholly typical, but within the twin anonymities of particular and general discovers a human identity.[1]

The heart of what is loosely called mysticism lies in experience which our capacity for solitude reveals. *Mystics claim to know the secret things of God disclosed in a particular way to their innermost selves, and then undertake to express their knowledge for the benefit of humanity at large.*[2] While stressing that the Kingdom of God is within, however, mystics deny that their experience is just subjective. As the familiar paradox maintains, God is transcendent and immanent, the soul-spark in each of us as well as the single goal outside us towards which we strive. When mystics write about such matters, they not surprisingly stress the inadequacy of words, though often using many words to do so, therefore depending on language to proclaim its limitations. And yet, although caught with something unutterably unique to say, mystics also reassure us that we are more alike with respect to the ineffable than we sometimes think. They remind us how, habitually and for practical purposes, we ignore the Spirit which is present in the immensely queer fact that we know at all. Attention to facts at the expense of attention to mental processes from which facts emerge, they tell us, blinds us to ourselves[3] and to that essential solitude 'wherein', as St John of the Cross says, 'the soul attains to union with the Word, and consequently to all

1

refreshment and rest'.[4] The ground sustaining our everyday acts of perception should itself therefore receive attention, even though we continually confound our efforts by bringing forward for analysis what lies anterior to analysis: the process of know-ledge, it seems, remains always richer and more strange than the mind can grasp or words can say.

'These deeds must not be thought/After these ways; so, it will make us mad', advises Lady Macbeth, who is, of course, herself incipiently mad, having (for practical purposes) murdered her king. Her aim is efficiency above all, and so she insists on seeing 'these deeds' objectively. In unlikely sympathy with her logic – and in language strangely echoing her condemnation of her husband's haunted desire to be 'founded as the rock' – Sir Karl Popper points out the futility of practical people (and he means especially scientists) being too introspective. 'The quest for certainty, for a secure basis of knowledge,' he writes, 'has to be abandoned'.[5] Of course Popper is correct: if everyone kept on defining terms, no work would get done, and definitions do not guarantee practical effectiveness. In this respect at least, he and Lady Macbeth are in accord. But the main, obvious difference between them the mystics would have us see first. On the one hand, things *must* be considered with the kind of introspection and self-scrutiny that might indeed make us mad, and in Lady Macbeth's derangement we see that subjectivity cannot without peril be neglected. Although her final state of mind parodies the wholeness induced by higher stages of contemplative prayer, it points to the same spiritual dimension of reality. On the other hand, despite their stress on subjectivity, mystics are empirical. Like Popper, they are not overconcerned with terms, and attend hardly at all to the formal word, 'mysticism'. If a vision is not testable, says the Irish mystic AE, ignore it:

> The religion which does not cry out: 'I am today verifiable as that water wets or that fire burns. Test me that ye can become as gods'. Mistrust it. Its messengers are prophets of the darkness.[6]

If character is not transformed, if good works do not follow, say the Christian saints, we are to doubt that we have had a religious experience. 'If you see a sick woman to whom you can give some help', writes St Teresa, 'never be affected by the fear that your devotion will suffer, but take pity on her: . . . . That is true union with His will.'[7]

Verification by works, however, is not the same thing as a scientist's empirical verification, and AE's statement must strike us as overambitious. The mystic, after all, talks about a God whom we cannot test as we can, say, the specific gravity of water. Yet the mystic's claim is not for that reason unconnected with the actual world, any more than concepts like 'beauty' and 'goodness' are meaningless because we cannot observe or handle or measure them directly. They are, rather, ideas which enable us to see ordinary things differently, with greater coherency and richness. 'God', as John Wisdom points out,[8] is a preposterous notion which calls for our serious investigation because it enriches experience, and because (as the mystics insist) such enrichment results in a transformation of character. The willingness of contemplative saints to be empirical thus compels our attention, even though we, and they, acknowledge that God, who is known first by faith, cannot be proved by empirical means.

Mystics, then, remain practical while asking that we consider the workings of our secret selves. Objective and subjective, particular and general, they maintain are reconciled finally in the Supreme Reality, the source and end of Being.[9] This they claim to know experimentally, just as they say that their special knowledge must be founded in faith and reflected in love for others, preserving such canons of mortality (and, Père Poulain adds, of science)[10] as men have found true. If mystical experience is to be tested, therefore, against moral and scientific wisdom, we must consider it a part of culture, and, in so doing, we face also the question of faith as a cultural phenomenon.

When we teach a child its colours by laying out an assortment of coloured threads, we are then at the mercy of the child's coming to see that some are blue and some yellow. Meanwhile we repeat the conventional sounds, suddenly become vacant in all their arbitrariness: 'blue', 'yellow'. Relief comes when the child takes up our sounds and points to the right threads, and within such a synthesis coming alive with meaning, lie the roots of faith without which there is no human truth.[11] The child takes us at our word in order to discover the meaning of discourse; just so, the mystics would take us back to a child's simplicity of faith, as they would have us see also beyond our worldly sophistications.

Whatever analysis one offers of mysticism's relation to culture will be, therefore, in the end, an analysis of faith and culture combined. Faith, because mysticism addresses the tacit dimensions of knowledge which we accept, like children, without knowing how; culture because it is the mirror in which we come to recognise, assess and communicate the quality of such faith. Clearly, we cannot keep apart, in some Cartesian manner, a subjective area within which to locate 'mystical experience', as distinct from an area of public knowledge or 'ordinary experience'. Faith itself is obscurely conditioned by culture, and mystics tend to meet the God described in their creeds; at any rate as far as we can tell from what they tell us.[12] All of which serves to confirm how finally irresolvable is the relationship of mysticism to tradition, so that it is futile to press for a solution exclusively in terms of either 'pure experience' or 'culture', as the following examples indicate.

The most influential, recent proponent of the contribution of 'culture' to mysticism is R. C. Zaehner. In *Mysticism Sacred and Profane* Zaehner denounces Aldous Huxley's claim in *The Doors of Perception*, that an experience induced by mescalin is equivalent to the Beatific Vision. This kind of uncritical syncretism, says Zaehner, is an insult to religion and an abuse of the accumulated wisdom of centuries of careful enquiry. Zaehner goes on:

While Huxley was still contemplating . . . ineffable realities, the investigator intervened and asked him about human relations. And here we come to a crucial and most important part of the experiment, as Huxley himself clearly saw. 'One ought to be able', he said, 'to see these trousers as infinitely important and human beings as still more infinitely important.' Unfortunately this was far from being the case: 'in practice it seemed impossible'.[13]

That grey flannel has its mysteries nobody denies. But insight into the nature of flannel that leaves the observer unconcerned about real differences between a man and his trousers seems spurious, somehow disappointing. It produces the same kind of feeling we have on learning from Darwin that his pursuit of science atrophied his ability to respond to poetry and the arts, and affected his capacity for friendship.[14] We feel uneasy that something, somewhere, went wrong. The same point comes to light, interestingly reversed, in an anecdote concerning Descartes who, in a fit of enthusiasm about a philosophical point, once slapped his patroness, Queen Christina of Sweden, on the thigh, after which she discreetly had a small table placed between them. Whereas with Darwin we worry that too much objectivity might diminish us personally, with Descartes we discover that the man was not, after all, as neatly divided as his philosophy. The activity of 'pure thought' does not, even for him, operate in isolation from the body-machine. The enthusiastic gesture redeems a human complexity that Descartes' theory simplifies, and shows us a fuller, more surprising dimension than we had expected. In some such way, people *are* richer, more surprising,[15] and more complexly involved in the world and in that web of attitudes and evaluations and institutions which we call culture, than are stones, or grey flannel, or scientific theories. Admittedly, there is a difference between mystical knowledge and the kind represented by Darwin and Descartes, but the claims of *sapientia* are rooted in *scientia*, and the highest mystics insist that their special knowledge is an illumination, or completion, of the ordinary knowledge which we all share, and not its negation. Zaehner is therefore right: something in Huxley desired keenly to escape the terrifying, painfully complex human clamour, and to flatten the extraordinary diversity of sacred and profane knowledge to his own preferred 'suchness'. The whole story of Huxley's battle with himself on this account, however, is not told in *The Doors of Perception*, and Zaehner does not relate it either.[16]

The main point remains: those who, with Blake, see heaven in a grain of sand, sometimes conclude too readily with Huxley (seeing heaven in a piece of flannel),[17] that *homo mysticus* is everywhere the same, that a 'perennial philosophy' stands at the heart of all religions, despite cultural differences, as a core of truth which we can isolate and test for ourselves.

Since the nineteenth century, growing sophistication in comparative studies of religion would seem, indeed, to encourage the perennial philosophers. Mankind being one, a careful search into what mankind, at its noblest, believes, should reveal some consensus: what rises might well converge, and in a sense it does. We can hear the Golden Rule in a variety of tongues; we are exhorted, perennially, to seek enlightenment and to avoid worldliness; at the root of religion we are asked to acknowledge a recurrent *mysterium tremendum et fascinans*.[18] There is good reason, in short, to affirm the enduring sameness and consistency of mystical teachings among the world's great religions.

In recent years, the journal *Studies in Comparative Religion* especially has given voice to a group of scholars who, with force and eloquence, have put the case for a proper understanding of this point of view. 'They were clearly men under authority', writes Jacob Needleman in their praise, 'to speak from an idea without veering off into apologetics and argumentation':[19] refreshing, yes, to have learned people discuss, without footnotes, how man is a metaphysical creature for whom the science of quantification does not account; how in the wonder of his intellect he can grasp at his own spiritual being, of which he finds a record in symbols shared by the world's great religions.

The doyen of this school is René Guénon,[20] a French orientalist who died a convert to Islam, and taught that a catastrophic downward spiral of Western civilisation began with the loss of a vital sense of metaphysics. Catholic Christianity had once sustained, in the West, a link to 'Primordial Tradition', now broken almost beyond hope of repair by a 'reign of quantity' introduced by the modern rise of science. Guénon holds out little hope for Western civilisation unless by a revitalising assimilation of Primordial Tradition from the East, where it is relatively unadulterated (though grievously threatened) by technology and empire-building.

Guénon writes with intellectual penetration and elegance. His central thesis commands attention, though it is scarcely novel; yet originality is Guénon's least concern. Truth is 'original', he claims, only if we take 'original' in a literal sense, for truth is now as always, and we can only repeat it, as the great religions have done from time immemorial. Guénon then posits an intellectual élite, who perennially detect the pure metaphysical content of 'original' truth, and he distinguishes these few from the masses immersed in worldly concerns on the plane of manifestation, receiving tradition through picture images and creeds.

Zaehner has harsh words for Guénon, mainly because the élitism seems arrogant.[21] By what authority, asks Zaehner, does Guénon presume to unravel critical and spiritual problems deriving from the course of entire civilisations? Such an endeavour is, like Huxley's, too simple, and retreats from particulars to an abstract, gnostic haughtiness.

To read Guénon's *The Crisis of the Modern World* is to feel most acutely the weight of Zaehner's reservations. What the intellectual élite knows, we are told, will be known, intuitively, to the intellectual élite, and Guénon refuses to express this knowledge further, or to proselytise by providing argument or evidence. Moreover, the entire enterprise of modern science and modern Western civilisation is denounced with disturbing confidence: ('"profane" science, the negation, that is to say, of true intellectuality'). From amidst the elegant prose we catch the enthralled gaze not seeing many of us at all, 'since it would be enough if there could arise a numerically small but firmly established élite to act as guides for the mass'.[22]

By contrast, however, Guénon's *Symbolism of the Cross* (trans. A. Macnab, London: Luzac, 1975), offers a compelling, imaginative, and beautifully organised analysis of a particular symbol, and Guénon's gifts appear here at their best. It could be argued that, by not considering this book, Zaehner fails fully to assess Guénon's achievement. Nevertheless, the central complaint in the long run seems correct: perennial philosophy conceived in terms of a superior intellectual caste tends to dwell in a rarefied air that scarcely nourishes common humanity. And yet, there is more to tell; for a favourite gesture of learned commentators who generally agree with Zaehner on this issue is in turn to rebuke him for being doctrinaire. In the preface to *Mysticism Sacred and Profane* Zaehner makes it clear that he is a Catholic; therefore he does not bring 'complete objectivity' (p. xiii) to bear on his subject. But the problem is not just belief; rather that Zaehner permits theological judgement to interfere with matters of classification. In his eagerness, for instance, to distinguish theistic mysticism (the crowning experience of which is the Christian Beatific Vision) from monistic mysticism (which identifies the soul or self with the divine, and teaches doctrines of absorption), Zaehner is insensitive to the real depth of religious experience in traditions which he opposes to his own. His eggs are in *two* baskets, one critic says, instead of many.[23]

It is easy to see that, brought to extremes, objections against the perennial philosophy tend also to be objections against the metaphysical roots of religious experience itself, which (Guénon is correct to say) we grasp intuitively, not by demonstration. At the opposite extreme (as Zaehner points out) lies an etiolated hauteur which disdains the rough embrace of particulars, confusing life with principles and reducing faces to physiognomy. General and particular, faith and experience, culture and perennial truth thus present themselves finally as polarities: on each side we encounter a boundary beyond which the analytical mind may not proceed, and yet the opposites cannot exist in separation, and call for synthesis. The most clear-headed writing on such subjects, consequently, will define the boundaries to present us finally with paradox, and thereby place the question of mysticism within limits of human discourse and, so, of culture. The *best* writing, however, will go on to invest such descriptive accuracy with a quality of personal perception, communicating a sense of how one manages to transcend paradox by dwelling within it in a human manner. An expression in language of this personal quality we can call *poetry*; expressed in action, as a mode of life concerned with the dialectic between experience and culture and with respect to man's ultimate values,[24] it is *mysticism*.

The mystic, to summarise, takes his stand within a radical act of acculturisation where reason calls on faith to enable the human acquisition of truth.[25] So placed, he knows as a child does, with simplicity and tentativeness, except that the mystic is more self-conscious than a child and remains deliberately open to mystery beyond the reach of analysis, intimated by that elusive, perpetually hidden communion of self and world, wherein personal judgement and evaluation are formed. Poised thus at the limits of reflection between subject and object, faith and experience, solitude and human community, the mystic has much in common with the poet, but with this difference: the poet is not essentially concerned with man's ultimate destiny, and the perfection he seeks is that of the poem he writes.[26] Likewise, the mystic is not essentially concerned with art, but pronounces his vision of an ultimate synthesis in the One Source of all manifestation, within which our partial creative efforts will be taken up and made whole. The mystic moreover claims to know something of this all-embracing synthesis by means of a special, abnormal venture in experience, wherein the secrets of God are encountered in a manner incommunicable through ordinary discourse. He therefore stresses two things: first, that we all have within us the seeds of mystical experience, which we detect by reflection on the fiduciary character of ordinary knowledge; second, that the spiritual energy which reflection discovers at the heart of language and culture is, in special states of contemplative prayer, illuminated in a glorious silence which language subserves, and mirrors imperfectly.

At this point, the crafty serpent of ineffability again twinkles at us. Mystics tell us they cannot say what they experience, though claiming just as firmly to have had fundamental insight into the nature of reality. Yet, again, reason holds firm to what it can. There is nothing unacceptable in writing about the way of silence in many words; no incompatibility in the hermit's embracing solitude for love of the city. Silence, after all, is understandable only to those who speak; solitariness to those whose nature is social; faith to those who have reason.[27]

Problems raised by ineffability rather have to do with knowing when to relinquish the pressure of reasoned enquiry, and when to apply it. One point against Zaehner is that he tends to move overhastily from descriptions of experience to generalising about experience itself, and in so doing he relinquishes reason too soon. But although Professor Smart criticises Zaehner for confusing theological belief with classification of documents, the professor wisely stops short of absurdities engendered by illusions that his own kind of argument can produce a final answer, and affirms what Zaehner began by confessing: understanding religious experience depends on commitment.[28]

This argument has insisted, therefore, on the futility of discussing mystical experience outside some framework of belief, and in subsequent chapters I confine myself to literature of mysticism in the Latin West, by which I mean a tradition extending, roughly, from St Augustine through the Western church of the Middle Ages, and into the modern scientific societies of Western Europe. I do so not for exclusionist reasons, but the reverse: this is the way which permits, for the present author, fullest articulation of the question. Still, one proceeds cautiously, for in Western tradition mysticism has not been officially defined, even though, as one commentator says, it is 'the truly dynamic element in the church',[29] and has consequently demanded careful appreciation. Madmen, after all, perennially attest that they walk with angels, the hysterical that they see God, fanatics that the Spirit leads their armies: and all these may speak true, or none of them, or some. As always, the disgusting, the magical, the spurious and superstitious bid to be taken seriously, whence has arisen a patient tradition of directing souls,[30] and of affirming those whose lives and writings seem to show forth the God whose nature the theologians and philosophers and lawyers describe in language appropriate to their enquiry.

Understandably, the church has often been uneasy with its mystics, because when false they are dangerous, and when true they are also dangerous because likely to proclaim the institution's inadequacy. For their part, the mystics are often uneasy with ecclesiastical authority, and anxious to avoid heresy. Their writings, consequently, are less a result of artistic aspiration or pathological confession or mere individualism, than the desire to bring forward, in order to examine and have examined and thereby clarified, the extraordinary thing they have encountered.[31] The process is co-operative, at once delicate and strenuous, requiring strength of intellect and subtlety of perception to embody the full simplicity of insight within a complexity of circumstances. By catching at something of this process in words, the great mystical authors have produced a literature maintaining the dialectic between a culture's articulate framework of reasoned enquiry, and vision that continues to outstrip it. Some such combination of effects can be seen especially to characterise the *Incendium Amoris*[32] of the English visionary, Richard Rolle (c.1300–c.1349), to which I now turn, in conclusion, as a means of drawing together the main ideas of this discussion.

It may surprise a modern reader to learn that during the two centuries after Rolle's death, he was much more widely read than Chaucer.[33] Part of the reason is that Rolle's audience had a livelier interest than moderns in devotional literature, but part lies also in Rolle's influence as a person of great sanctity, and in his distinction as a writer.[34]

Though not unorthodox, Rolle was a maverick.[35] As a young man, he left Oxford without a degree, donned a habit of his own devising, made from his sister's clothes (she reportedly thought him mad), and became a hermit. Through his example, and by means of voluminous writings in English and Latin, Rolle's authority grew. At the time of his death, there was a cult of 'St Richard, Hermit', and a group of nuns at Hampole, anticipating his canonisation, prepared an office to be read on his saint's day. The canonisation did not occur, but neither did devotion to Rolle's writings abate.

The *Incendium Amoris*, with the *Melos Amoris*, contains most clearly Rolle's teachings on mystical experience. The *Incendium* was written c.1340, some ten years after the *Melos*, and twenty years after Rolle's conversion. It is more rounded and satisfying than the earlier work, and shows a temperament mellower than that of the young enthusiast who, in *Judica me, Deus* (before 1322), undertook sharply to castigate abuses of ecclesiastical office.

The main teachings of the *Incendium Amoris* are clear, and frequently repeated through the forty-two chapters of the long version. We must turn our heads in faith towards God, and away from things of the world which are means, at best, to bring us to our supernatural end. We should expect to receive the heavenly gift of contemplation only after a long and disciplined personal effort of preparation, which includes loving our neighbour. We must avoid extremes and use good sense in matters of mortification, never forgetting the 'law of common humanity' (p.122). We must hope to make continual progress towards perfection in this life, and towards the supreme mystery which we will never fully know in its essence. We can grasp only inadequately through language the contemplative splendour with which a few are blessed.

As a work of literature, the *Incendium* of course offers more than is contained in a summary of its contents. In Chapter 15 Rolle tells, for instance, how he became aware of an interior 'symphony of song' which put him out of tune with the psalms he was trying to repeat, and how, through the interior melody, came a taste of divine fire: 'Then and there my thinking itself turned into melodious song, and my meditation became a poem . . . . The effect of this inner sweetness was that I began to sing what previously I had spoken; only I sang inwardly, and that for my Creator' (p.93). Several times Rolle describes thought suddenly becoming melodious (pp.177, 121, 164). He talks also of the contemplative's prayer being truly musical because recited 'with a certain spiritual quality' (p.114).[36] This effect, turning thought towards music, is the very distinction of poetry, and Rolle, grasping the point, attempts to show through the music of language something of the Spirit's work. His constant appeal to a threefold metaphor of heat (*calor*), sweetness (*dulcor*), and music (*canor*), is his primary means to this end. 'Fundamentally', he says of true contemplatives, 'they know nothing within themselves but spiritual heat, heavenly song, divine sweetness' (p.60).

The threefold pattern is at first clearly placed before us, but Rolle explores interpenetrations among the three elements by concentrating now on one, now on another. Even though in normal experience we can feel heat, sweetness and music with alarming acuteness, they are often sensed in a diffuse manner, and this fluctuation between soft and hard focus, which is true to experience, enables Rolle's analysis itself to shift and flow without strain, now exploring the most nebulous spiritual stirrings, now rising to rapturous intensities. The Latin prose is characteristically heavy with alliteration and mobile with rhythmic exuberance, qualities which often distract us from the pattern, but inevitably we are swung round, back to the three things needful 'above all else . . . warmth and song and sweetness' (pp.88–9).

The effect is at once to suggest design, but not prescription, so that dynamic thinking never crystallises into stable thought. Heat, sweetness and what Rolle calls 'song' are highly generalised. Rolle, for instance, dissociates 'song' from its outward expression as sound: rather, the term seems to indicate what Wallace Stevens means by 'Music is feeling, then, not sound', or what Jacques Maritain indicates by those 'inaudible psychic charges of images and emotion' which represent the first stirrings of creative intuition, and which he calls music, or *mousike*.[37] Yet fluid interrelationships between Rolle's three elements are formed also to embody a particular autobiography, and so to communicate the development of a particular mind. The emergent yet indistinct patterning, the stable yet fluid structure express insight into the working of a particular human consciousness which no abstract account alone could contain.

The 'poetic' or literary effect of Rolle's prose comes, therefore, from interplay between a singular identity of experience and its manifold relevance for humanity at large. The true contemplative, we learn, discovers a 'pattern' (p.78), whereas sinners are 'very feeble. Their love has no pattern' (p.51). The spiritual man's heart is 'fixed' (p.78) in Christ, and Rolle repeatedly insists on the desirability of order, discipline and form. Consequently, we are invited to discover stable patterns in the writing which can suggest order and sense of direction, distinguishing the true contemplative from the 'chorus' of mere worldlings.

For instance, at the conclusion of Chapter 5, Rolle had introduced his three 'fundamentals', but, before turning to Chapter 6, on the Trinity, paused to warn us against 'unbridled curiosity' (p.61). We seem at once to be encouraged by the very placement of the discussion of the Trinity in Chapter 6, to find correspondences involving threefold patterns, and yet we are warned *against* being too curious or ingenious. The chapters on the Trinity are doctrinally orthodox: their 'pattern' in this respect is predictable. However, the language of sweetness and harmony is interwoven with exposition in a manner which prevents us from schematising the doctrine too easily. 'There is nothing so sweet as loving Christ' (p.64), Rolle writes. In the 'Father's home there will be clearer light if we bring our whole heart to the loving of God. We shall all be *taught of God* and so will rejoice in wonderful harmony'. Here the Son clearly is associated with sweetness, and the Father with harmony. But there is no suggestion, in these chapters, that the Spirit is fiery, even though elsewhere in the book the association is explicit: 'Thus it happens that when the fire of the Holy Spirit really gets hold of the heart it sets it wholly on fire and, so to speak, turns it into flame' (p.101).[38] We are not, therefore, wrong to complete the pattern which Chapter 6 suggests but leaves tantalisingly incomplete: the Son *is* sweetness, the Father *is* song, and the Spirit *is* heat.

It is intriguing to apply such Trinitarian schemes to other parts of the book: for instance, to Rolle's treatment of diffusion, unity and transformation (p.101), or to the pattern in reverse, as world, flesh and devil (pp.98, 180). But lest we suspect ourselves of 'reading in' too enthusiastically, Chapter 31 provides a rationale for Rolle's consistent suggestion of inexact correspondences.

While describing his gift of spiritual song, Rolle rebukes those who 'tried to make me conform to their pattern' (p.142), and concludes that 'I have had a soul differently ordered' (p.142). Different, and yet not entirely so, for we are told soon after that all the saints 'hasten in the same direction', even though taking 'different paths' (p.159). We are advised frequently to make progress in spiritual life according to our capacity, and we are also warned to respect moral laws that bind us to our neighbour. Rolle therefore is interested both in attesting the validity of his own experience, which does not quite conform to a pattern, and in making clear that part of this validation lies in his convincing the reader that the particular favour of God's grace has not set him apart altogether from his fellows, or from the general community of orthodox opinion. Throughout the *Incendium*

Amoris the man of examined faith therefore stands before us no less than the enthusiast. Rolle has read the Bible and the Fathers, and is familiar with scholastic debate.[39] Offsetting the auto-biographical account, which is the story of one man's eccentric course, is the continuing witness to that same man's learning and intelligent use of tradition, both scholastic and rhetorical,[40] which helps him to clarify the content and discover the meaning of his experience.

The moralist, the man of insight, individualist, scholar, disciplinarian and visionary are unified by a highly energised authorial voice. We are given not merely thought, but 'thinking' that is 'surging up into spiritual song' (p.121), and which presents us with a single quality of language and spirit, containing and synthesising the diverse, but eminently human capacities of the man himself, facing his God. Rolle warns us against resting in things which are 'only imagination' (p.145), and requires us to know that reading a book like the *Incendium Amoris* is no substitute for living well. But in moving us to appreciate that 'musical' energy which breathes life into the conventional forms of language and thought, he introduces us to a realm of mind wherein the impulses of artistic creativity and spiritual life lie closely intertwined. That Rolle's experience has been judged to fall short of the heights of contemplation need not detain us here: it seems he knew neither the Dark Night of the soul, nor the state of highest union, and his contemporaries seem to have had reservations about the overaffective caste of his thought.[41] Such questions are valid, and it is well to know about them, as examples of tests which tradition and culture can bring to bear on a particular vision and quality of faith. But my emphasis has been on how the *Incendium Amoris* suggests that if the *via mystica* is to be expressed in language, the language of poetry is the most complete, most satisfactory, analogue for the delicate equilibrium of faith and personal experience lived in the context of a culture both nourishing and testing. Those that have ears to hear, let them hear, for 'Those who love the world indeed know the words or verses of our songs, but not their music' (p.192).

TEXTS WITHOUT COMMENT

1 MYSTICISM, FAITH AND CULTURE

SOLITUDE AND ISOLATION

1. For the rest, nothing more is enjoined you, my brethren, but the solitude of mind and of spirit. You are alone in this way, when you exclude the thought of common things, and all attachment to present things; when you contemn what the many admire, and count as nothing what they eagerly covet; when you avoid disputes, make light of temporal losses and forget injuries. Otherwise, you will not be really alone, even when you have no visible company. Or do you not understand that one can be alone although surrounded by a multitude and, contrariwise, one can be in the company of many when exteriorly alone? You are alone, my brethren, no matter what number are with you, provided you are careful neither to inquire too curiously into the conduct of your neighbour, nor rashly to sit in judgment upon his doings. And if you happen to discover some fault in him, even so, beware of condemning, but rather excuse.

   Bernard of Clairvaux (1091–1153),
   Sermons on the Canticles, XL

2. Whosoever of you hath not this in his conscience, showeth it not in his life, practiseth it not in his cell, he should be called not solitary but desolate; nor is his cell a cell to him, but a prison and a dungeon.

   William of St Thierry (1085–1148),
   The Golden Epistle, IV, 9

3. The greatest Saints avoided the society of men when they could: and rather chose to serve God in secret. One said. As oft as I have gone among men: I returned home less a man. This we often find: when we talk long together. It is easier not to speak a word at all: than not to speak a word too much. It is easier to hide at home: than to be guarded abroad.

   Thomas à Kempis (1380–1471),
   Of the Imitation of Christ, Bk. I, Ch. 20

4. 'And in solitude hath she built her nest.' The previous solitude of the soul was its voluntary self-privation of all the

comforts of this world, for the sake of the Bridegroom – as in the instance of the turtle-dove – its striving after perfection, and acquiring that perfect solitude wherein it attains to union with the Word, and in consequence to complete refreshment and repose. This is what is meant by 'nest'; and the words of the stanza may be thus explained: 'In that solitude, wherein the Bride formerly lived, tried by afflictions and troubles, because she was not yet perfect – there, in that solitude, hath she now fixed her nest, because she has found perfect rest in God.'

John of the Cross (1542–91),
Spiritual Canticle, stanza xxxv

5. Others err worse that cease not to reprove and slander solitary life, saying: *Vae soli*; that is to say: 'Woe be to a man alone'; not expounding 'alone' as 'without God', but 'without a fellow'. He truly is alone with whom God is not.

Richard Rolle (c. 1300–49),
The Fire of Love, Ch. xiii

6. Love forsooth dwells in the heart of the solitary if he seeks nothing from vain lordship. Here he utterly burns and longs for light whiles he thus clearly savours things heavenly; and sings with honey-sweetness and without heaviness; as the seraphim – to whom he is like in loving mind – cries and says to his noble Lover: 'Behold, loving, I burn; greedily desiring.'

Richard Rolle (c. 1300–49),
The Fire of Love, Ch. xiv

7. I was asked this question: Some people shun all company and like to be alone, their peace depends upon it, would they not be better in the bosom of the church? I said, No, and you shall see why. The righteous man is righteous still in any place and any company and the unrighteous man is unrighteous still in every place and in all company. The righteous man has God in truth in him. But one who has God in very truth will have him in all places, in the streets and in the world no less than in the church, in the desert or the cell: if he has gotten him indeed and gotten him alone he is proof against all hindrance.

Meister Eckhart (1260–1327),
In Collationibus, 6, 'Solitude and God-getting'

KNOWING AND DOING

8. None can say worse of God, than that his invitations are not in earnest.

> Bénjamin Whichcote (1609–83),
> *Select Notions*, 'Apostolical Apothegms', 23, 4

9. But if a creature is to comprehend and to understand God, it must be caught up beyond itself into God, and comprehend God with God. Whosoever then would know and understand what God is – which is not permitted – he would go mad. Behold, all created light is powerless to know what God is. What God is in Himself, transcends all creatures; but that God exists, is testified by nature, and by Holy Writ, and by every creature.

> John of Ruysbroeck (1293–1381),
> *Adornment of the Spiritual Marriage*, Ch. XXI

10. The powers of the soul cannot attain to this divine ground; and the great wastes to be found in this divine ground have neither image, nor form, nor condition; for they are neither here nor there. They are like unto a fathomless abyss, bottomless and floating in itself. Even as water ebbs and flows, up and down, now sinking into a hollow, so that it looks as if there was no water there, and then again, in a little while, rushing forth as though it would engulf everything, so does it come to pass in this Abyss. This, truly, is much more God's Dwelling-place than heaven or man. A man, who verily desires to enter in, will surely find God here, and himself simply in God, for God never separates Himself from this ground. God will be present with him, and he will find and enjoy eternity here. There is no past or present here; and no created light can reach unto or shine into this divine ground; for here only is the Dwelling-place of God and His sanctuary. Now this Divine Abyss can be fathomed by no creatures; it can be filled by none, and it satisfies none; God only can fill it in His Infinity. For this abyss belongs only to the Divine Abyss, of which it is written: *Abyssus abyssum invocat.*

> John Tauler (c. 1300–61),
> Sermon, 'On the Feast of the Nativity of
> St John the Baptist'. The Second Sermon

11. What then is the *abyss* that calls, and to what other 'abyss'

does it call? If by 'abyss' we understand a great depth, is not man's-heart, do you not suppose, *an abyss*? For what is there more profound than that 'abyss'? Men may speak, may be seen by the operations of their members, may be heard speaking in conversation: but whose thought is penetrated, whose heart seen into? What he is inwardly engaged on, what he is inwardly capable of, what he is inwardly doing, or what purposing, what he is inwardly wishing to happen, or not to happen, who shall comprehend? I think an 'abyss', may not unreasonably be understood of man, of whom it is said elsewhere, Man shall come to a deep heart, and God shall be exalted.

> Augustine of Hippo (354–430),
> On Psalm XLI, 13

12. As little as a Piece of Work can apprehend him that made it, so little also can Man apprehend and know God his Creator, unless the Holy Ghost enlightens him; which happens only to those that rely not upon themselves, but set their Hope, Will, and Desires only upon God, and move in the Holy Ghost, and these are one Spirit with God.

> Jacob Boehme (1575–1624),
> *Aurora*, 2, 24

13. And the overwhelming joy made him ill. The man thought to himself and said: 'Who are you that you should be filled with such overwhelming joy?' He sat for a long while in thought, and the more he thought the less he could understand what had happened. Then he decided to write about these things as he had been commanded. But all his senses and reason could not express what he had seen; no words could describe it. Then he thought of expressing it in pictures and formulas; but again he could not, for it was beyond all pictures and formulas. Then he thought he would reason about it and reach by reason and concepts; but it was beyond all reason and all human concepts. The more he thought about it the less he knew, because it was greater than anything he had ever seen or heard of. This amazed him and he said: 'O Beloved, tell me what thou meanest. Thou saidst I had to see the origin and then write about it so that men could conceive it. Now thou hast made me see such a great wonder that I cannot express it in words. I have tried with all my reason, but no word will describe it. Nor can I

describe where I have been or what I have seen and heard, except for one thing: that I know my heart and my soul are full of an overwhelming joy which frightens me, for I know it will be hard to control.'

The answer came: 'You must do it as far as you can, because men nowadays refuse the divine gifts, not knowing what they are'.

Rulman Merswin (c. 1310–82),
Book of the Nine Rocks

14. And when I looked, I beheld God who spake with me. But if thou seekest to know that which I beheld, I can tell thee nothing, save that I beheld a fulness and a clearness, and felt them within me so abundantly that I can in no wise describe it, nor give any likeness thereof.

Angela of Foligno (1248–1309),
The Book of Divine Consolation, III, 2

15. Grace alone can teach it, nor can it be learned save by experience. It is for the experienced, therefore, to recognise it, and for others to burn with the desire, not so much of knowing, as of feeling it; since this canticle is not a noise made by the mouth but a jubilee of the heart, not a sound of the lips but a tumult of internal joys, not a symphony of voices but a harmony of wills. It is not heard outside, for it sounds not externally. The singer alone can hear it, and He to Whom it is sung, namely, the Bridegroom and the Bride. For it is a nuptial song, celebrating the chaste and joyous embraces of loving hearts, the concord of minds, and the union resulting from reciprocal affection.

Bernard of Clairvaux (1091–1153),
Sermons on the Canticles, I

16. But in this question of seeing God, it seems to me that there is more value in one's manner of living than in his manner of speaking.

William of St Thierry (1085–1148),
Enigma of Faith, 3

17. Remember, then, that all rational creatures have their own vine indeed, but it is joined directly to their neighbour's vine, so closely that no one can do good or harm to his neighbour without doing it to himself.

Catherine of Siena (1347–80),
The Dialogue, 'A Treatise on Discretion', XXIV

18. When I see people very anxious to know what sort of prayer they practise, covering their faces and afraid to move or think lest they should lose any slight tenderness and devotion they feel, I know how little they understand how to obtain union with God since they think it consists in such things as these. No, sisters, no; our Lord expects *works* from us. If you see a sick sister whom you can relieve, never fear losing your devotion; compassionate her; if she is in pain, feel for it as if it were your own and when there is need, fast so that she may eat, not so much for her sake as because you know your Lord asks it of you. This is the true union of our will with the will of God.

Teresa of Avila (1515–82),
Interior Castle, Fifth Mansion, III, 11

19. Judge not therefore of your Self, by considering how many of those Things you do, which Divines and Moralists call Virtue and Goodness, nor how much you abstain from those Things, which they call Sin and Vice. But daily and hourly, in every Step you take, see to the Spirit that is within you, whether it be Heaven, or Earth that guides you, And judge every Thing to be Sin and Satan, in which your earthly Nature, own Love, or Self-seeking has any Share of Life in you.

William Law (1686–1761),
The Spirit of Love, Dialogue I

20. The first is that love ought to manifest itself in deeds rather than in words.

Ignatious Loyola (1491–1556),
Spiritual Exercises, Fourth Week, 'Contemplation for Obtaining Love,'

21. That which instructs us is what happens from one moment to another producing in us that experimental science which Jesus Christ Himself willed to acquire before instructing others. In fact this was the only science in which He could grow, according to the expression of the holy Gospel; because being God there was no degree of speculative science which He did not possess. Therefore if this experimental science was useful to the Word incarnate Himself, to us it is absolutely necessary if we wish to touch the hearts of those whom God sends to us.

Jean-Pierre de Caussade (1675–1751),
Abandonment to Divine Providence, I, ii, 8

22. And if it happen (as many times and to too often it doth) that
     thou be troubled or disquieted, by any sodain assault, al
     other things set aside, attend first of al to pacifie thy mind,
     for that beeing quiet, many things are done, and wel done
     and without this, thou canst not do any thing of any value;
     besides that, thou dost thereby lye open to the blowes of
     thine enemies. The divell dooth so much feare this peace (as
     a place where God doth dwell for to woorke therein
     woonders) that oftentimes with the banners or ensignes of a
     friend he attempteth to deceive us with inspirations, which
     in apparance are good, stirring up in us a sundry good
     desires. The deceit whereof is knowne by the effects,
     because they take from us the peace of our harts.

                                        Lorenzo Scupoli (1530–1610),
                                        The Spiritual Conflict, 16

FAITH AND UNDERSTANDING

23. The difficulty of believing is rather a signe of Vocation, than
     the easinesse.

                                        Juan de Valdes (1490–1541),
                                        Considerations, XXIX

24. The very obscurity of faith is an argument of its perfection.
     It is darkness to our minds because it so far transcends their
     weakness. The more perfect faith is, the darker it becomes.
     The closer we get to God, the less is our faith diluted with
     the half-light of created images and concepts. Our certainty
     increases with this obscurity, yet not without anguish and
     even material doubt, because we do not find it easy to subsist
     in a void in which our natural powers have nothing of their
     own to rely on. And it is in the deepest darkness that we
     most fully possess God on earth, because it is then that our
     minds are most truly liberated from the weak, created lights
     that are darkness in comparison to Him; it is then that we are
     filled with His infinite Light which seems pure darkness to
     our reason.

     In this greatest perfection of faith the infinite God Himself
     becomes the Light of the darkened soul and possesses it
     entirely with His Truth. And at this inexplicable moment

the deepest night becomes day and faith turns into understanding.

Thomas Merton (1915–68),
New Seeds of Contemplation, 134–5

25.   True Faith is the Might of God, one Spirit with God; it
worketh in God and with God.

It is free, and bound to no Articles, but only to the right
and true Love, wherein it draws the Breath of its Life's
Power and Strength, and lies not in human Arbitrium,
Opinion, or Conjecture.

For as God is free from all Inclination or Deviation, so that
he does what he will, and need give no Account for it, so also
is the true Faith free in the Spirit of God; it has but one
Inclination, viz. into the Love and Mercy of God, that it cast
its willing into God's willing; and to go out from the
Syderial and elementary Reason.

It seeks not itself in the Reason of the Flesh, but in God's
Love; and so if it thus finds itself, then it finds itself in God,
and co-worketh with God, not as to Reason, what that
wills, but in God, what God's Spirit wills.

For it prizes or esteems not the earthly Life, but that it may
live in God, and that God's Spirit in it may be the Willing
and the Doing; it gives up itself in humility into God's
Willing, sinks through Reason into Death, and yet springs
with God's Spirit into the Life of God. It is as it were not,
and yet is in God in all.

It is a Crown and Ornament of the Deity; a Wonder in the
divine Magia: it makes where nothing is, and takes where
nothing is made: it works, and none sees its Substance.

It lifts up itself aloft, and yet needs no climbing up; it is
very Mighty, and yet is the most lowly Humility of all; it
hath all, and yet comprehends nothing more than Meekness, and so it is free from all Evil.

And it hath no Law, for the fierce Wrath of Nature
touches it not: it subsists in eternity, for it is comprehended
in no Ground; it is included or Bolted up in nothing.

As the Abyss of Eternity is free, and rests in nothing, but
only in itself, where there is an eternal Meekness, so also is
the right true Faith in the Abyss.

It is in itself the Substance: it liveth, and yet seeks not its
own Life, but it seeks the Life of the eternal still Rest: it goes

forth out of its own Life's Spirit, and possesses itself.

Thus it is free from the Source of Torment, and dwells thus in the eternal Liberty in God.

Jacob Boehme (1575–1624),
A Treatise of the Incarnation, III, 6–16

26. For understanding is the reward of faith. Therefore do not seek to understand in order to believe, but believe that thou mayest understand.

Augustine of Hippo (354–430),
Homilies on the Gospel of John, XXIX, 6

27. The more hidden the divine operation beneath an outwardly repulsive appearance, the more visible it is to the eye of faith.

Jean-Pierre de Caussade (1675–1751),
Abandonment to Divine Providence, I, ii, 2

28. In the next place, since our opponents keep repeating those statements about faith, we must say that, considering it as a useful thing for the multitude, we admit that we teach those men to believe without reasons, who are unable to abandon all other employments, and give themselves to an examination of arguments; and our opponents, although they do not acknowledge it, yet practically do the same. For who is there that, on betaking himself to the study of philosophy, and throwing himself into the ranks of some sect, either by chance, or because he is provided with a teacher of that school, adopts such a course for any other reason, except that he *believes* his particular sect to be superior to any other?

Origen (c. 185–253),
Against Celsus, I, 10

29. Let life follow in the tracks of death; let light travel in the path of darkness; and let the antidote of truth enter by the same door as the poison of the old serpent, and heal the eye, which is 'troubled', in order that it may serenely contemplate Him Who is inaccessible to trouble. So let the ear, which was the first gate open to death, be also the first open to life. Let the hearing, which was the means of destroying the sight, be made the means of its restoration; because unless we believe we shall not be able to understand. Consequently, merit belongs to hearing, and reward to sight.

Bernard of Clairvaux (1091–1153),
Sermons on the Canticles, XXVIII

30. I speak boldly yet truly, that an infidel liveth not without faith: for if I demand of him, who is his father or mother, straightways he will tell me, such a man and such a woman: and if I press him further, whether he doth remember the time when he was first conceived, or the hour when he was born into this world, he will answer me, that he never knew or saw any such thing: and yet for all this doth he believe that which he never beheld, seeing he believeth, without all doubt, that such a man was his father, and such a woman his mother.

> Gregory the Great (540–604),
> *The Dialogues*, Bk. IV, Ch. 2

31. Wherefore I give Thee thanks, my God, because Thou makest plain to me that there is none other way of approaching Thee than that which to all men, even the most learned philosophers, seemeth utterly inaccessible and impossible. For thou hast shown me that Thou canst not be seen elsewhere than where impossibility meeteth and faceth me. Thou hast inspired me, Lord, who art the Food of the strong, to do violence to myself, because impossibility coincideth with necessity, and I have learnt that the place wherein Thou art found unveiled is girt round with the coincidence of contradictories, and this is the wall of Paradise wherein Thou dost abide. The door whereof is guarded by the most proud spirit of Reason, and, unless he be vanquished, the way in will not lie open. Thus 'tis beyond the coincidence of contradictories that Thou mayest be seen, and nowhere this side thereof.

> Nicholas of Cusa (1401–64),
> *The Vision of God*, IX

CHAPTER TWO
Imagination and Mystery

Imagination abides in ambiguity, its glory and liability: 'twofold Always', says Blake, 'May God us keep/From single vision, and Newton's sleep!'[1] The attack on Newton is for confusing nature congealed into matter with the whole of nature, thereby causing Spirit to sleep. But to attend to Spirit only, and ignore one's place in the world, is to risk a debilitating indifference. Tranquillity found merely by emptying one's self 'of every image and of all activity', writes John of Ruysbroeck (1293–1381) in his attack on the quietist Beghards, leads to a state of suspension, a 'bare vacancy' which is the 'beginning of all ghostly error'.[2]

The characteristic *modus operandi* of human knowledge mediating between Spirit and Matter, in what Ruysbroeck calls an active or loving 'self-mergence', we may presume to call 'Imagination'. Through it, the human soul declares most fully its middle state. And yet, the mystics assure us that their highest insights cannot be rendered in images: man, it seems, does not live by imagination alone. 'Thus by degrees', writes St Augustine, 'I passed from bodies to the soul . . . withdrawing itself from those troops of contradictory phantasms that so it might find what that light was, whereby it was bedewed'.[3] Dionysius the Areopagite, whose treatise *Mystical Theology* assumed an almost canonical authority in the later Middle Ages, has made the classical statement of this teaching on the insufficiency of images:

For the more that we soar upwards the more our language becomes restricted to the compass of purely intellectual conceptions, even as in the present instance plunging into the Darkness which is above the intellect we shall find ourselves reduced not merely to brevity of speech but even to absolute dumbness both of speech and thought.[4]

Images drawn from experience of the corporeal world, we learn repeatedly, are inadequate, and fall away before the radiance of divine darkness. But, as Charles Williams points out, this 'Negative Way', which purges the inadequacies of imagination, is offset by and implies an 'Affirmative Way', which, with equal justification, considers all that is vital in imagination as a trace of divinity:

> The one Way was to affirm all things orderly until the universe throbbed with vitality; the other to reject all things until there was nothing anywhere but He. The Way of Affirmation was to develop great art and romantic love and marriage and philosophy and social justice; the Way of Rejection was to break out continually in the profound mystical documents of the soul, the records of the great psychological masters of Christendom. All was involved in Christendom, and between them, as it were, hummed the web of ecclesiastical hierarchy, labouring, ordering, expressing, confirming, and often mis-understanding, but necessary to any organization in time . . . .

These two approaches, Williams insists, do not exist in isolation, because 'No Affirmation could be so complete as not to need definition, discipline, and refusal; no Rejection so absolute as not to leave necessary (literally and metaphorically) beans and a wild beast's skin and a little water. Those who most rejected material things might cling the more closely to verbal formulae; those who looked most askance at the formulae might apprehend most easily the divine imagery of matter.'[5] The material world, in short, is somehow to be taken up into God through contemplative vision, and not denied, even if voluntarily rejected in certain circumstances.

Affirmative and negative attitudes to imagination must therefore be distinguished carefully from abuses which dog them closely. Images are neither to be glorified for their own sake, nor despised. Kierkegaard describes such a twofold aberration as leading to a twofold despair: that of the wishful thinker who pursues a rare bird of imagination until he is lost in the forest at nightfall without companions, and that of the melancholic for whom imagination provides no possibility other than dread. On the one hand, those who live by imagination alone, divorced from intellect, lack purpose, but those who deny the images risk falling into vacancy. For the self is a synthesis,[6] Kierkegaard concludes, by which he means an equilibrium of forces held open to higher meaning, like Williams' balance of Affirmative and Negative. Not surprisingly, in his passage on withdrawing from sensuous images, St Augustine continues by assuring us that his glimpse of 'That which is' does not imply disparagement of the mind's congress with created things: 'And then I saw Thy invisible things understood by the things which are made'. Augustine appeals here to St Paul (Romans, 1:20), in whose curious, intransigently liberal voice Christian theology might be said first to have taken form. Preaching 'Jesus Christ, and him crucified' (1 Cor.: 2, 2), St Paul found in the language (and some of the ideas) of Greece, a ready vehicle for the sublime paradox in which Western imagination came most fully to appraise the human relationship to God. Invisible things of eternity are known, obscurely but truly, in the things of creation: Christ had not disdained human flesh, nor should we. Rather we should make use of circumstances at our disposal to pursue the invisible things, the mysteries, through things that are made; that is, by way of imagination.

When St Augustine as a young man schooled in Latin rhetoric and with a smattering of Greek philosophy, in near despair in a garden at Milan, took up and read St Paul, he came to understand something of the apostle's vision of how invisible things are mirrored by the things of time, and thereby laid the foundation for his own mature writing, the most influential of the West's formulations of religious faith. As Augustine well knew, the Hebrews, among whom graven images were forbidden, held fast to God's transcendence; yet they insisted on this remote God's care for his chosen ones. As the hills 'stand about Jerusalem; even so standeth the Lord round/about his people', a protector and Father whose 'loving kindness is comfortable', but who treads under his feet 'all them that depart from thy statutes' (Ps. 119). The psalmist speaks for a nation whose terrible glory has been to encounter God in the unique, linear and unrepeatable course of history.

For Greek philosophy, it was otherwise. Plato's *Timaeus* tells that time is an image of eternity, whose mysterious light is stained by the multiform catastrophe of Ideas having found physical embodiment. Still, the higher may be detected truly, if imperfectly, in the lower. Consequently Plato, like all those who think deeply about imagination, is in two minds about it. In the *Republic,* poets are banished because they are secondhand imitators of Forms, and give us a copy of things which are themselves copies of eternal Ideas. Nevertheless, the poets are slipped in at a crucial juncture of Plato's argument to provide a myth serving to unite the will of the Republicans, enlivening them, however high or low their caste, to ideals to which the state aspires.

In the *Ion,* Plato speaks of poets in another sense altogether. As inspired seer (not just imitator) the poet brings insight from a higher-than-ordinary source, and this, in a way, is the effect achieved by the (inspired) author of the *Republic,* so that we are left to meditate the spectacle of a poet, Plato himself, whose very sense of the power of poetry leads him to denounce it.

Of course it is incorrect to deal with Plato as if he were discussing some discrete, post-Romantic view of poetic imagination. Nevertheless, it remains clear that he is concerned mainly with images in context of how material things in space reflect their originating principles. For the Greeks in Plato's tradition, the mind's images, like those in literature, are valuable because, by the nature of things, the One cannot help being reflected through the multivalent world of becoming. However, Plato also insists that the One, like ideal Goodness, cannot be adequately described from this world's perspective.

By contrast, Judaic tradition concentrates on time, and on the unique processes of history, eschewing attempts to see material things as, somehow, copies of divine Ideas. For the Hebrews, the God of philosophers determined to become manifest as a matter of principle, is at best simply foreign. And yet Hebrew poetry, despite its emphasis on God's transcendence, remains full of human tenderness and anguish, celebration and grief, emotions which express the Almighty's solicitude, directing Israel's destiny.

In each case, the same theme is stated; there is inexpressible mystery, yet images have a part to play in awakening us to it. Plato, like the Psalmist, though with a different emphasis, at once affirms imagination as an approach to the divine, and yet rejects it as insufficient. For Western Christendom, of course, the meeting of Plato and the Psalmist – of Greek philosophy, that is, and Hebrew religion – was formative, and it lay especially with St Augustine to interpret the major possibilities which this extraordinary confluence of cultures offered in the person of Jesus Christ, in whom the eternal *Logos* declared itself in a timely moment, unique and unrepeatable.

The *Confessions* therefore presents Christ as *Logos* in a Greek manner, and, also, in language of the psalms, as a human incarnation of the Father's love and care for humankind. Augustine's prose is at once passionate ('nor can man's hard-heartedness thrust back Thy hand . . . and nothing can hide itself from Thy heat' [v, 1, 1]), and analytical ('for sooner could I imagine that not to be at all, which should be deprived of all form, than conceive a thing betwixt form and nothing, neither formed, nor nothing, a formless, almost nothing' [XII, vi, 6]). In a famous passage he declares:

> My weight, is my love; thereby I am borne, whithersoever I am borne. We are inflamed, by Thy Gift we are kindled; and are carried upwards; we glow inwardly, and go forwards. We ascend thy ways that be in our heart, and sing a song of degrees; we glow inwardly with Thy fire, with Thy good fire, and we go; because we go upwards to the peace of Jerusalem. (XIII, ix, 10)

The fire of charity, God's gift, burns from the heart to enliven humanity. But in the philosopher's language, weight is also described as a body finding its proper place in the 'degrees' of the chain of being: appropriately, fire rises and tends, as does love, towards our proper home, the heavenly Jerusalem, a city not of this world, but of eternity which time mirrors, for which all nature groans, and which all things reflect according to their 'reasons'.

It is a cliché to accuse Augustine of not having the philosophy of his theology, but it is unfair to require of his special synthesising energies some kind of post-Kantian sophistication. Augustine, rather, gives us a vocabulary and a way of thinking about the relationship between imagination and mystery which remained fundamental to further thought on the subject throughout the Latin Middle Ages.[7] Certainly, the 'troops of contradictory phantasms' of which he complains are often an impediment to highest vision, but the Word, he assures us, was made incarnate, and can be recognised in creation and through the words and deeds of men. Angels, not humans, are privileged with 'intellectual vision', the capacity to 'read without any syllables in time, what willeth Thy eternal will' (XIII, xv, 18). Such spiritual 'sight' is sometimes available to human beings in this life, though they cannot rest in it, only glimpse the mysterious splendour before resuming life in an ordinary world, where knowledge is by faith, and mediated through images.

On the lowest level, antithetical, so to speak, to intellectual vision, Augustine tells us that normal human knowledge must involve an interaction between body and object, a process which he describes as 'corporeal vision'. Augustine denied that body could modify spirit, and, so, we might say, corporeal vision manifests the activity of spirit on the level of perception. But the human mind's most characteristic activity is to mediate between 'corporeal' and 'intellectual', acknowledging the world of physical nature, yet knowing by intuition the higher reasons operative within it. This activity Augustine calls 'spiritual vision', and it is close to what we mean by 'imagination'.[8] 'Christian reality', writes a modern critic of Augustinian thought, 'was neither the Platonic dream of a disembodied logos, an intellectual reality totally divorced from the world, nor an unintelligible nightmare irredeemably lost *in* the world: it was rather, like syntax, time pressed into the service of eternity.'[9]

Through Augustine's own acts of imagination, the language of charity and pilgrimage, of marriage and separation, of the degrees of knowledge and the loss of Eden, of heavenly Jerusalem and earthly Babylon, the higher reason and the lower, of active and contemplative lives, of faith that precedes understanding, of the threefold vision, and a robust philosophy of time that would redeem time for eternity by dwelling in it faithfully: all this would remain close to the heart of contemplative literature in Western tradition. And although epistemological problems of a modern sort did not preoccupy Augustine, within the theory of 'spiritual vision' we find an intuition about the twofold nature of imagination which continues to be taken up by modern minds. As Martin Buber writes in the opening sentence of *I and Thou*: 'To man the world is twofold, in accordance with his twofold attitude. The attitude of man is twofold, in accordance with the twofold nature of the primary words which he speaks'.[10] Buber's primary words are *I-Thou* and *I-It*, for 'I' cannot be spoken alone, but either in relation to, or distinction from, what is addressed. The curious binary status of ordinary knowledge mediating between Matter and Spirit, we continue to acknowledge long after Augustine because the fact remains so strange and compelling. Perception itself, we come to recognise, takes hold of the world unbidden, charged obscurely with meaning. And we know ourselves to perceive because we can attend to the difference between perceiving and thinking, a fact which it seems impossible to deny, sensibly. As the consistent sceptic, seeking, like most men, the security of a place to rest, elevates his denial of absolutes itself into an absolute, so scepticism about attention participates in the process the sceptic would deny.[11]

But attention, though self-authenticating, is indeterminate: we attend always *to* something, even though our object is indefinite, as when a puzzling configuration of colour and shape seizes on us when we are half awake, and continues to puzzle us until, fully awake, we can name it, and it falls back into place among the bedroom ornaments. A scarlet curtain blowing in the wind can terrify an infant because attention is filled with a furious quality which the mind cannot 'place'. Children's jokes delight in such puzzles enacting the comprehension of perceived qualities within concepts. 'What's red and green and goes one hundred miles an hour?' A frog in a food-processor.[12]

We call upon attention, therefore, as Maurice Merleau-Ponty says, to save the objective world.[13] Consciousness alone does not constitute things, for, if it did, things would lose their recalcitrance, their resistance to our attentive gaze: but if there were only things there would be no power of attention. Within such a synthesis we are to grasp the sense of 'spiritual vision', and the movement of imagination within which we are required to dwell. Further reflection draws us merely to some miracle of immediate apprehension, a point at which we encounter the world, joined to it, yet able to hold it at a distance. While we are, so to speak, in the automobile we cannot see under the bonnet, but because the engine works, we had just as well get on with driving. So, by the exercise of imagination we are invited to experience a world filled with signs and wonders: 'the countenance of creation is a great book. Behold, examine, and read this book from top to bottom'.[14]

Since Augustine's time, however, it has become less clear in what manner the world *is* a book. Problems involved in mediaeval theories of mind's apprehension of 'Ideas' or 'Forms' in created nature gave rise to an avalanche of contemptuous rebuke at the hands of philosophers during the seventeenth and eighteenth centuries. We are not likely, now, to proceed unwitting of their criticism, even though the cost of such scrutiny was to take the imaginative life out of ideas, and to relegate God to the transcendental designer's studio of the Deists.[15] By reaction, the Romantics made explicit, once more, that imagination, as witness to the mind's subjective but creative congress with things, is a bearer of truth and not just an impediment to clear thought. But by focusing on the inner dynamics of the image, Romanticism encouraged poetry increasingly to take its own process as its subject, so that Romanticism has, consequently, been less successful in constructing a theology commensurate with its psychological insight.[16] But as one result of such a development, we can assess more clearly than St Augustine some key differences between poets and mystics; that is, between imagination as a quality of literature aiming to express beautifully the self's psychic relationship to things, and as a quality of life directing the self, through Spirit, towards God.

A certain set of terms now confronts us: *Matter*, that of which we are conscious, as Coleridge says, and which is not conscious itself; *Spirit*, which operates in the openness to experience which we know through the fact of our limitations imposed by Matter, and in our partial freedom from such limitations; *Imagination*, the characteristic psychic life of man, a power of apprehension and of synthesis in which, as Wordsworth says, 'bodily eyes/Were utterly forgotten, and what I saw/Appeared like something in myself'.[17]

As Coleridge recognised, Wordsworth took 'primary imagination' as his theme: that is, the primordial, creative contact of the human mind and nature. But in the very act of thus thematising 'primary imagination', Wordsworth's poetry makes clear the gulf that can exist between capturing such experience in words and following out its consequences theologically, as the mystics advise. With the decline of his creative powers after the great decade of 1798–1808, Wordsworth's life-story remained complex and energetic, but it was not a story of private turmoil finding direction through contemplative vision and 'heroic virtue'. Wordsworth, we might conclude, was a poet, but not a saint, and Bertrand Russell's quip on the subject catches the main distinction:

> In his youth he [Wordsworth] sympathized with the French
> Revolution, went to France, wrote good poetry, and had a
> natural daughter. At this period, he was a 'bad' man. Then he
> became 'good', abandoned his daughter, adopted correct prin-
> ciples, and wrote bad poetry.[18]

The point is worth stating (even with such archness), not to serve
some rankling perfectionism that would demand our poets be
saints and *vice versa*, but rather the reverse: it enlivens us to the
variety of human vocations, and to the fact that division of labour
is a condition of mental life as it is of other forms of human work,
and that not everyone can be a high mystic. For St Augustine
such distinctions would be less evident, partly because he had
more faith that phenomena were themselves full of divine significance which we are called upon to interpret, and which lead us to
God. And yet the fact remains that a modern reader can
appreciate the *Confessions* for its imaginative power and intellectual scope without feeling compelled to believe a word of it.
We are simply more prepared than Augustine to distinguish
between words and deeds, language and belief.

Standing between St Augustine and ourselves, with respect to
such distinctions, is Edmund Spenser's *Faerie Queene*. The last
completed part, Book VI, we could say remains 'Augustinian'
and yet sufficiently close in time to Prince Hamlet's self-
scrutinising awareness of language to enable Spenser to register
poignantly something of how the mystery of imagination,
which poetry declares, is distinguishable from the imagination of
mystery which the saints claim should direct our conduct.

Sir Calidore, in Book VI, is Spenser's knight of courtesy,
which Spenser describes as virtue's fairest flower:[19] extravagant
praise, one feels, for a mode of behaviour commonly thought of
as something close to etiquette. But courtesy has a special
meaning. We learn that there are no explicit rules governing it;
rather, it requires a sense of discernment commensurate with
poetry itself, and stands in relation to the rules of decorum as
does the virtue of poetry to the rules of prosody. Courtesy,
simply, is the poetry of conduct, at once distinct from literature,
and yet analogous to it. Once Spenser had made such a point,
exhorting his readers to fashion their lives like a poem, he con-

tinued the *Faerie Queene* no further.

We have no clear reason why Spenser stopped writing when he did, but Book VI seems to complete and complement Book I, where Spenser attempted to write poetry about holiness, virtue's fairest flower in another sense. Poet and saint thus find themselves at last in complementary opposition. In Book I, we are asked to acknowledge both that holiness is the aim of all virtues, and also that poetry cannot describe holiness completely. In Book VI, we learn that the heart of virtue (the empirical test of holiness, as it were) lies in conducting ourselves in a manner analogous to a poem, though knowledge of poetry alone does not enable us to do so. Spenser seems thus to believe imagination can introduce us to mystery, but poetry pronounces also its separateness from life, even though, with a master's insight, Spenser refuses to admit, finally, a divorce: Sir Calidore's most serious, because undefeatable, enemy is the Blatant Beast, a monstrous rumour-mongering distorter of *words*. Calidore, after all, in fashioning his life with a poet's craft, is not to be let free from the poet's entanglement with language, if only because the distortion of words can cause misdirected action.

For St Augustine, the world of the book is co-extensive with the book of the world, and both direct us towards God. Although Augustine well knows that the words in both books have limitations, he is not overconcerned about differences between the kind of contemplation that follows upon interpreting words, and interpreting things. A good deal of this old faith remains in Spenser, but is disturbed by a more pressing awareness that the tasks of poet and saint, though overlapping, are distinct, and not quite commensurate. And how we pursue such a line of enquiry will force us to resolve the question of mysticism's relation to imagination, because the central difference between poet and saint, as we have seen, has to do with the *ends* to which they direct their curiously symbiotic yet distinct activities.[20] For the poet, 'words alone are certain good',[21] as Yeats declares, and the poet's aim is to produce a work of art, bringing to life through language an encounter between himself and things, the act in which intelligibility itself arises, full of wonder and strangeness. The poet celebrates the natural miracle of significance: consequently, a poem cannot be reduced to its 'theme', which is a disenchanted, if true, statement, as it were, after the fact. Shakespeare, for instance, has Othello declare:

> I had rather be a toad
> And live upon the vapour of a dungeon
> Than keep a corner in the thing I love
> For others' uses
>
> (III, iii, 296 ff.)

We may describe Othello's words as expressing jealousy, and we would not be incorrect: poetry remains intelligible. But had Othello said 'I am jealous', we would value Shakespeare's art less. In the difference between our declared theme and the impact of Shakespeare's language, lies the poetry. It *gives* us jealousy, as a violent gesture gives us anger. We do not first register the gesture in our minds, and then interpret it: we register *this anger*. Similarly, in Othello's words the nexus of subterranean, reptilian and covert things, the claustrophobia and vindictive hugger-mugger, well up with the force of complex and disturbing emotion which has a grip on us before we name it, 'jealousy'.

The mystic's experience is distinct from the poet's because the mystic is concerned, not just with the work of art produced, but with producing his life as a work of art dedicated to God. Mystics of course are alive in the world and amidst the manifold being that poets affirm, so that the mystic's 'art', like the poet's, cannot be reduced to a set of themes. The mystic, however, traverses the world's multiplicity to unite with the Absolute that gives rise to it, and is beyond words. As St Augustine says, our experience in time is like syntax, the meaning of which is revealed in silence which comes with the end of the sentence. Such silence is not empty, but gathers the words into understanding: so is the mystic silence of the Negative Way beyond imagination, but it does not deny the affirmations poets make. The Irish mystic AE, whose friendship with W. B. Yeats presents a remarkable example of the relationship between poet and saint, once wrote about his friend, and described the main difference between them: the poet, says AE, dwells in the many mansions of heaven, while the mystic, who is 'interested more in life than the shadows of life'[22] seeks 'the real nature of one who has built so many mansions'.

Mystics, therefore, who have experienced 'the real nature of the One', not surprisingly tend towards the Negative Way, and warn against timebound philosophies identifying their ends too closely with material goals. Poetry, for its part, awakens us to mystery through beauty, but does not satisfy our hunger. 'There is no excellent beauty', says Francis Bacon, 'that hath not some strangeness in the proportion'.[23] Poignancy that irradiates the truly beautiful and rends the heart, warns that in art is no final resting place, but a promise of life: *inquietum cor est nostrum, donec requiescat in te.* The poet therefore deploys imagination at first affirmatively, to celebrate the world and its myriad incarnate brilliance. But it is fruitless to search in the works of artistic imagination for convincing proof that their author has had direct experience of the Absolute which mystics proclaim is beyond words and which literature approaches, thus, indirectly. St Teresa of Avila, mystic first and author only by constraint, does not claim that her experiences prove God's existence, but concludes: 'If anyone thinks I am lying I beseech God, in His Goodness, to give him the same experience'.[24] Pascal, author first and then mystic, tells us he experienced God in an extraordinary manner, but his record of the event is halting and inelegant:

Dieu d'Abraham, Dieu d'Isaac, Dieu de Jacob,
Non des philosophes et des savants.
Certitude. Certitude. Sentiment. Joie. Paix.[25]

Evelyn Underhill detects in Pascal's stylistic failure an indication that the experience was genuine:

Compare with the classic style, the sharp and lucid definition of the 'Pensées', the irony and glitter of the 'Provinciales', these little broken phrases – this child-like stammering speech – in which a supreme master of language has tried to tell his wonder and his delight. I know few things in the history of mysticism at once more convincing, more poignant than this hidden talisman; upon which the brilliant scholar and stylist, the merciless disputant, has jotted down in hard, crude words, which yet seem charged with passion – the inarticulate language of love – a memorial of the certitude, the peace, the joy, above all, the reiterated, all-surpassing joy, which accompanied his ecstatic apprehension of God.[26]

What comes through, certainly, is the critic's enthusiasm and radiant faith. But the bare fact that Pascal's style stumbles can in no manner assure us that the author had seen God, any more than

St Teresa's literary account of her experiences will convince a sceptic.

England's greatest poet, whose work portrays every kind of human type except the mystic, shows us, in one place especially, how the threshold lies between imagination and mystery. At the end of *A Winter's Tale*, Hermione, abused wife of the tyrannical King Leontes, is restored to him after sixteen years. Contrite and repentant, Leontes is invited by his wife's loyal servant, Paulina, to view a life-size statue of Hermione whom he believes dead, and who, indeed, seems also to us to have died of grief sixteen years previously. In the play's most famous scene, as the characters stand in silence, the statue comes alive.

This wonderful conclusion strikes us in a number of ways, simultaneously. As we see the statue, we experience an agonising hope that, somehow, the man and his wife will be re-united. And indeed they are. The play then concludes with Paulina promising explanations afterwards, and immediately we begin on our own account to ponder what such explanations may be. Hermione, we surmise, had not died, but lived in seclusion for sixteen years until this moment when reconciliation with Leontes would be most perfect and most wonderful. But our reasonable explanation makes a most peculiar story out of the play's action, and especially the part Paulina plays in it. Perhaps, it occurs to us momentarily, Hermione did die, and we witness, with Leontes, the miracle itself. That, of course, offends reason because we do not rush at the miraculous when there is evidence for an alternative solution. Yet the miraculous claims us because of our desire that Hermione *should* be restored. Even if a statue must be brought alive to do it, the rightness of such a conclusion would answer our profound wish, beyond reason.

We misread the poetry if we do not feel *both* that the play shows us it contains its own reasons, and yet that the profoundest beauty arises from the images awakening in us a desire, and a poignancy, that the literature does not undertake to explain, and which both opens out upon the mystery of divinity (by way of Apollo's oracle), and in upon the mystery of ourselves. Shakespeare leaves us at the point where imagination calls upon faith, knowing that imagination cannot prescribe faith's content.

As the poet leaves us, then, to contemplate mystery, the mystic, who begins with such contemplation, in the end also affirms the poet's task. Mary Magdalene is, traditionally, the saint of contemplatives, and the legend tells of her life of devotion leading her to a house at Loreto, where she enjoyed the bliss of mystical marriage, her soul's union with God. The better-known part of the story recounts her anointing her Lord's feet with precious ointment, and suffering the rebuke of certain apostles (Matt.: 26, 8). The incident is not without bearing on her contemplative vocation, for, traditionally, it is taken to mean that she did not eschew the works of artistic imagination (represented by her anointing), which have their own necessary blessedness:

> The woman from Magdala in her golden hair, wasting her own time and the party funds: an embarrassment if not a scandal. But an act which is of the very essence of *all* poetry and, by the same token, of any religion worth consideration.[27]

Poets assure us that life cannot be lived by dogma or routine, or in an attitude of denial, but in a complex rhythm, perennially surprising. The mystic assures us that there is an end worth striving for, a silence in which the promises of imagination are fulfilled.

TEXTS WITHOUT COMMENT

2 IMAGINATION AND MYSTERY

IMAGINATION

1. There are three kinds of visions. The first is material, the second spiritual, the third intellectual. The first is of matter and with form; the second is without matter but with form; the third is without matter or form. The first conceives elemental things, the second imagined things, the third is not circumscribed in any way whatever.

   Richard of St Victor (–c. 1173),
   Commentary on Joel

2. And after this I saw God in a Point, that is to say, in mine understanding, – by which sight I saw that He is in all things.

   Julian of Norwich (1343–after 1413),
   Revelations, III, 11

3. Also in this He shewed me a little thing, the quantity of an hazel-nut, in the palm of my hand; and it was as round as a ball. I looked thereupon with eye of my understanding, and thought: What may this be? And it was answered generally thus: It is all that is made. I marvelled how it might last, for methought it might suddenly have fallen to naught for little[ness]. And I was answered in my understanding: It lasteth, and ever shall [last] for that God loveth it. And so All-thing hath the Being by the love of God.

In this Little Thing I saw three properties. The first is that God made it, the second is that God loveth it, the third, that God keepeth it. But what is to me verily the Maker, the Keeper, and the Lover, – I cannot tell; for till I am Substantially oned to Him, I may never have full rest nor very bliss: that is to say, till I be so fastened to Him, that there is right nought that is made betwixt my God and me.

Julian of Norwich (1343–after 1413),

Revelations, I, 5

4. To this faithful servant, as he is taken round, there would also be shown the storehouse of the royal silver, another for the gold, also for precious stones, for pearls, for different necklaces, one place too for the royal purple, another for the crowns. Besides he would be shown the queen's bedsteads, situated in several different apartments. But all these would not be fully displayed to him, with doors thrown wide open, but only with doors ajar, so that he could recognise indeed his lord's treasures and the wealth of the king, but not obtain clear and complete information of these various objects.

And afterwards this servant, who has been so trusted that his lord the king has made him acquainted with the vast extent of his possessions, would be sent to assemble an army for the king, to hold a levy and inspect the troops. By reason of his fidelity, in order to obtain more men for service and to assemble a more numerous army for the king, he will find it necessary to publish in part what he has seen. Yet also, by reason of his wisdom, knowing that it is necessary to hide the king's secret, he will rather make use of hints than of full descriptions. There will be no hiding of the king's power, yet the details of the arrangement and decoration of the palace and its plan will remain undivulged.

Origen (c. 185–253),

Commentary on Romans, V, 1

5. God is entirely one and single. But our Saviour, because the world is manifold, since God purposed Him to be the propitiation and first fruits of all creation, becomes many things, becomes perhaps anything, according as the whole creation capable of being set free has need of Him.

Origen (c. 185–253),

Commentary on John, I, 20

6. From all this it follows that since the creation of the world His invisible attributes are clearly seen . . . being understood through the things that are made; and so those who pay no heed to this and fail to recognize, praise, and love God in all these things, are without excuse, for they refuse to be brought out of the darkness into the marvelous light of God.

Bonaventure (1221–74),

The Journey of the Mind of God, II, 13

7. Everybody knows how difficult or almost impossible it is for the carnal mind still untaught in spiritual studies to raise itself to the understanding of unseen things and fix its eye upon contemplating them. For so far it knows nothing but bodily things; nothing presents itself to its thoughts but what it is accustomed to thinking about, that is visible things. It seeks to see invisible things and nothing meets its eye but the form of visible objects; it desires to consider incorporeal things but dreams of the images of corporeal things only. What shall it do then? Is it not better to think somehow about these things rather than to give up and neglect them? Indeed if the soul loves truly it will not easily forget them, yet it is much more difficult to rise up and contemplate them. Let it do what it may and think of them as it is able. Let it think through the imagination since it cannot yet by the pure intelligence. This is, I think, why Rachel first had children through her handmaid before she gave birth herself; for it is sweet for her to think upon them through the imagination when she cannot yet have an intelligent understanding by the reason. As we mean reason by Rachel, so we mean the imagination by her handmaid. Therefore the reason persuades us that it is better to think about the good things in some way or other and at least to kindle the soul with desire for them through imagining their beauty, rather

than to fix the mind upon false and deceptive goods. And this is the reason why Rachel wished to give her handmaid to her husband. Everybody unless he is quite inexperienced, knows that this is the first road towards contemplation of invisible things for a beginner.

> Richard of St Victor (–c. 1173),
> *Benjamin Minor*, 14

8. *Sacramentum* means a sign. That man never gets to the underlying truth who stops at the enjoyment of its symbol; and the seven sacraments all point us to the same reality.

> Meister Eckhart (1260–1327),
> *Sermons and Collations*, LXXVI,
> 'Ascension Day Sermons', 1

9. The spirit once tasted, all flesh fayleth.

> Benet of Canfield (1520–1611),
> *Rule of Perfection*, II, 5

10. Insomuch that when thou weenest best to abide in this darkness, and that nought is in thy mind but only God, if thou look wisely thou shalt find thy mind not occupied in this darkness, but in a clear beholding of some thing beneath God. And if it thus be, surely then is that thing above thee for the time, and betwixt thee and thy God. And therefore purpose thee to put down such clear beholdings, be they never so holy nor so liking. For one thing I tell thee: it is more profitable to the health of thy soul, more worthy in itself, and more pleasing to God and to all the saints and angels in heaven – yea! and more helpful to all thy friends, bodily and ghostly, quick and dead – such a blind stirring of love unto God for himself, and such a secret setting upon this cloud of unknowing, and thou wert better to have it and to feel it in thine affection ghostly, than to have the eyes of thy soul opened in contemplation or beholding of all the angels or saints in heaven, or in hearing of all the mirth and melody that is among them in bliss.

> *The Cloud of Unknowing* (late 14th C.), Ch. 9

11. Enkindled with the fire of divine Love, and entirely liquefied, the soul passes into God, is united to Him without any medium, and becomes with Him one spirit, even as gold and brass are welded into one mass of metal.

> Franciscus Ludovicus Blosius (1506–65),
> *The Book of Spiritual Instruction*, XII, 2

12. Guide us to that topmost height of mystic lore which exceedeth light and more than exceedeth knowledge, where the simple, absolute, and unchangeable mysteries of heavenly Truth lie hidden in the dazzling obscurity of the secret Silence, outshining all brilliance with the intensity of their darkness, and surcharging our blinded intellects with the utterly impalpable and invisible fairness of glories which exceed all beauty! Such be my prayer; and thee, dear Timothy, I counsel that, in the earnest exercise of mystic contemplation, thou leave the senses and the activities of the intellect and all things that the senses or the intellect can perceive, and all things in this world of nothingness, or in that world of being, and that, thine understanding being laid to rest, thou strain (so far as thou mayest) towards an union with Him whom neither being nor understanding can contain.

> Dionysius the Areopagite (c. 500),
> *The Mystical Theology*, I

ATTENTION

13. One of the two is only a little piece of flesh, naked, inert, and bleeding beside a ditch; he is nameless; no one knows anything about him. Those who pass by this thing scarcely notice it, and a few minutes afterward do not even know that they saw it. Only one stops and turns his attention toward it. The actions that follow are just the automatic effect of this moment of attention. The attention is creative. But at the moment when it is engaged it is a renunciation. This is true, at least, if it is pure. The man accepts to be diminished by concentrating on an expenditure of energy, which will not extend his own power but will only give existence to a being other than himself, who will exist independently of him. Still more, to desire the existence of the other is to transport himself into him by sympathy, and, as a result, to have a share in the state of inert matter which is his.

> Simone Weil (1909–43),
> *Waiting for God*, 146–7

14. When attention seeks prayer it finds it. For if there is anything that marches in the train of attention it is prayer; and so it must be cultivated.

Evagrius Ponticus (345–99),
Chapters on Prayer, 149

15. And this movement of the heart is not unsuitably illustrated by the comparison of a mill wheel, which the headlong rush of water whirls round, with revolving impetus, and which can never stop its work so long as it is driven round by the action of the water: but it is in the power of the man who directs it, to decide whether he will have wheat or barley or darnel ground by it. That certainly must be crushed by it which is put into it by the man who has charge of that business.

John Cassian (c. 360–435),
Conferences, I, 18

16. For the mind cannot love itself, except also it know itself; for how can it love what it does not know? Or if any body says that the mind, from either general or special knowledge, believes itself of such a character as it has by experience found others to be, and therefore loves itself, he speaks most foolishly. For whence does a mind know another mind, if it does not know itself?

Augustine of Hippo (345–430),
On the Trinity, IX, iii, 3

17. Friend,
Be still and cool in thy own mind and spirit from thy own thoughts, and then thou wilt feel the principle of God to turn thy mind to the Lord God, whereby thou wilt receive this strength and power from whence life comes to allay all tempests against blusterings and storms. That is it which moulds up into patience, into innocency, into soberness, into stillness, into stayedness, into quietness up to God with his power. Therefore mind, – that is the word of the Lord God unto thee, – that the authority and thy faith in that to work down, for that is it which keeps peace, and brings up the witness in thee that hath been transgressed, to feel after God who is a god of order and peace with his power and life. When transgression of the life of God in the particular the mind flies up in the air, and the creature is led into the night, and nature goes out of his course, and an old garment goes

on, and an uppermost clothing, and nature leads out of his course, and so it comes to be all of a fire in the transgression, and that defaceth the glory of the first body.

George Fox (1624–90),
Book of Miracles, 17

18. A third and most Sublime Degree of Attention to the Divine Office is, that whereby Vocall Prayers doe become mentall: that is, wherby soules most profoundly and with perfect simplicity united to God, can yet without any prejudice to such union, attend also to the sence and spirit of each passage that they pronounce; yea thereby find their affection, adhesion and union increased and more simplified. This Attention comes not till a soule be arrived to perfect Contemplation, by meanes of which the spirit is so habitually united to God, and besides, the imagination so subdued to the spirit, that it cannot rest upon any thing that will distract it.

Augustine Baker (1575–1641),
Sancta Sophia, Treatise III, 14

19. For while we are in sight of, we are not yet one with, what we see. While we notice any thing we are not one with it. Where there is no more than one no more than one is seen: God is not seen except by blindness, nor known except by ignorance, nor understood except by fools. According to St Augustine, no soul can get to God who goes not without creature and seeks not God without likeness. And that is the meaning of Christ's words, 'Cast out first the beam out of thine own eye and then wash the mote out of another's eye'.

Meister Eckhart (1260–1327),
Sermons and Collations, LXXVI,
'Ascension Day Sermons', 1

20. The reason why the inward silence is so necessary is because this is a proper disposition, and is requisite for receiving into the soul the Word, which is the eternal and essential speech. It is a well known truth that in order to receive the outward Word, we must give ear and hearken. The sense of hearing is made for receiving the Word, which is spoken or communicated to it. The hearing is a sense more passive than active; it receiveth, but doth not communicate. And because the internal essential Word desireth to speak within the soul, and to communicate itself to, and revive and quicken it, it is

absolutely necessary that the soul be attentive.
Madame Guyon (1648–1717),
A Method of Prayer, XIV

WORDS AND SILENCE

21. There are three kinds of Silences; the first is of Words, the second of Desires, the third of Thoughts. The first is perfect, the second more perfect, and the third most perfect.
Miguel de Molinos (1640–97),
The Spiritual Guide which Disentangles the Soul, I, xvii, 128

22. A certain member of what was then considered the circle of the wise once approached the just Anthony and asked him: 'How do you ever manage to carry on, Father, deprived as you are of the consolation of books?' His reply: 'My book, sir philosopher, is the nature of created things, and it is always at hand when I wish to read the words of God'.
Evagrius Ponticus (345–99),
Praktikos, 92

23. I cannot write nor do I wish to write – but I see this book with the eyes of my soul and hear it with the ears of my eternal spirit and feel in every part of my body the power of the Holy Spirit.
Mechthild of Magdeburg (1212–99),
Revelations, Part 4, 13

24. Now, albeit this Dialogue passe not betwixt God and the sowlle in these expresse and formall tearmes, yet silently and in spirit they passe in effect and substance within the sowlle in this her desire of Humiliation; the which spirituall effect a man cannot espresse but by such articulate words.
Benet of Canfield (1520–1611),
Rule of Perfection, II, 4

25. All the things of which I have spoken, when compared with that of which I am assured in my intelligence, so far as I am able to comprehend it in this life, are of such intensity, that, by the side of them, all things seen, all things felt, all things imagined, all things just and true, seem to me lies and things of naught. I am confounded at my inability to find stronger words. I see that God is in such perfect conformity with the

soul, that when He beholds it in the purity wherein it was created by His Divine Majesty He imparts a certain attractive impulse of His burning love, enough to annihilate it, though it be immortal; and in this way so transforms the soul into Himself, its God, that it sees in itself nothing but God, who goes on thus attracting and inflaming it, until He has brought it to that state of existence whence it came forth – that is, spotless purity wherein it was created. And when the soul, by interior illumination, perceives that God is drawing it with such loving ardour to Himself, straightway there springs up within it a corresponding fire of love for its most sweet Lord and God, which causes it wholly to melt away.

> Catherine of Genoa (1447–1510),
> *Treatise on Purgatory*, IX

26. God is a short word that has a long meaning.

> John Tauler (c. 1300–61), Sermon,
> 'On the Feast of St Andrew the Apostle'

27. They indeed may sound forth words: but they cannot give the Spirit. Beautifully do they speak: but if Thou be silent they kindle not the heart. They teach the letter: but Thou openest the sense. They bring forth mysteries: but Thou unlockest the meaning of sealed things. They declare Thy commandments: but Thou helpest to fulfil them. They shew the way: but Thou givest strength to walk in it. What they do is all without: but Thou instructest and enlightenest the heart. They water outwardly: but Thou givest fruitfulness. They cry aloud in words: but Thou impartest understanding to the hearing.

> Thomas à Kempis (1380–1471),
> *Of the Imitation of Christ*, Bk. IV, Ch. 2

28. Nothing causeth so much illusion in the interior Life, as the indiscreet choosing of Books.

> Francois Fenelon (1651–1715),
> *Maxims of the Saints*, II, 87

29. I may exist on after physical life is suspended, or I may not. No demonstration is possible. But what I want to say is that the alternatives of extinction or immortality may not be the only alternatives. There may be something else, more wonderful than immortality, and far beyond and above that idea. There may be something immeasurably superior to it.

As our ideas have run in circles for centuries, it is difficult to find words to express the idea that there are other ideas. For myself, though I cannot fully express myself, I feel fully convinced that there is a vast immensity of thought, of existence, and of other things beyond even immortal existence.

> Richard Jefferies (1848–87),
> *The Story of My Heart*, Ch. VIII

30. The Father uttered one Word; that Word is His Son: and He utters Him for ever in everlasting silence, and the soul to hear It must be silent.

> John of the Cross (1542–91),
> *Spiritual Maxims*, 284

31. That which we most require for our spiritual growth is the silence of the desire and of the tongue before God, Who is so high: the language He most listens to is that of silent love.

> John of the Cross (1542–91),
> *Spiritual Maxims*, 285

32. All strong rocks are broken here; all on which the spirit can rest must be done away. Then, when all forms have ceased to exist, in the twinkling of an eye, the man is transformed. Therefore thou must make an entrance. Thereupon speaks the Heavenly Father to him: 'Thou shalt call Me Father, and shalt never cease to enter in; entering ever further in, ever nearer, so as to sink the deeper in an unknown and unnamed abyss; and, above all ways, images and forms, and above all powers, to lose thyself, deny thyself and even unform thyself.' In this lost condition, nothing is to be seen but a ground which rests upon itself, everywhere one being, one life. It is thus, man may say, that he becomes, unknowing, unloving and senseless. This is not the result of natural qualities, but of the transformation, wrought by the Spirit of God in the created spirit, in the fathomless lost condition of the created spirit, and in his fathomless resignation.

> John Tauler (c. 1300–61), Sermon, 'On the
> Feast of St Matthew, Apostle and Evangelist'

TIME AND ETERNITY

33. And therefore take good heed unto time, how thou spendest

it; for nothing is more precious than time. In one little time, as little as it is, may heaven be won and lost. A token it is that time is precious: for God, that is giver of time, giveth never two times together, but each one after other. And this he doth because he would not reverse the order or the appointed course in the causes of his creation. For time is made for man, and not man for time. And therefore God, who is the ruler of nature, would not in his giving of time go before the stirring of nature in man's soul; the which stirring is even according to one time only. So that man shall have no excuse against God in the Doom, and at the giving account of the spending of time, saying thus: 'Thou givest two times at once, and I have but one stirring at once'.

The Cloud of Unknowing (late 14th C.) Ch. 4

34. For, in the mutual relations of the Persons in the Godhead, this contentment perpetually renews itself, in a new gushing forth of love, in an ever new embrace within the Unity. And this takes place beyond Time; that is, without before and after, in an eternal NOW. For, in this embrace in the Unity, all things are consummated; and in the gushing forth of love, all things are wrought; and in the life-giving and fruitful Nature lie the power and possibilities of all things. For in the life-giving and fruitful Nature, the Son is in the Father, and the Father in the Son, and the Holy Ghost in Both. For It is a life-giving and fruitful Unity, which is the home and the beginning of all life and of all becoming. And so all creatures are therein, beyond themselves, one Being and one Life with God, as in their Eternal Origin.

John of Ruysbroeck (1293–1381),
The Book of Supreme Truth, Ch. x

35. Yet they strive to comprehend things eternal, whilst their heart fluttereth between the motions of things past and to come, and is still unstable. Who shall hold it, and fix it, that it be settled awhile, and awhile catch the glory of that ever-fixed Eternity, and compare it with the times which are never fixed, and see that it cannot be compared; and that a long time cannot become long, but out of many motions passing by, which cannot be prolonged altogether; but that in the Eternal nothing passeth, but the whole is present; whereas no time is all at once present: and that all time past, is driven on by time to come, and all to come followeth

upon the past; and all past and to come, is created, and flows
out of that which is ever present? Who shall hold the heart of
man, that it may stand still, and see how eternity ever still-
standing, neither past nor to come, uttereth the times past
and to come? Can my hand do this, or the hand of my mouth
by speech bring about a thing so great?

Augustine of Hippo (345–430),
Confessions, XI, 13

36. That any thing may be found to be an infinit Treasure, its
Place must be found in Eternity, and in Gods Esteem. For as
there is a Time, so there is a Place for all Things. Evry thing
in its Place is Admirable Deep and Glorious: out of its Place
like a Wandering Bird, is Desolat and Good for Nothing.
How therfore it relateth to God and all Creatures must be
seen before it can be Enjoyed. And this I found by many
Instances. The Sun is Good, only as it relateth to the Stars, to
the Seas, to your Ey, to the feilds, &c. As it relateth to the
Stars it raiseth their Influences; as to the Seas it melteth them
and maketh the Waters flow; as to your Ey, it bringeth in the
Beauty of the World; as to the feilds; it clotheth them with
Fruits and flowers: Did it not relate to others it would not be
Good.

Thomas Traherne (1637–74),
Centuries, III, 55

37. Even so the mind, unsatisfied with this infernal light, will
scale the firmament and search the heavens to find the breath
that spins them, the heavens by their revolution causing all
things on earth to grow and flourish. Its spirit never rests
content until it pierces to the coil, into the primal origin
where the breath has its source. This spirit knows no time
nor number: number does not exist apart from the malady
of time. Other root has none save in eternity, where there is
no number except one. This spirit, transcending number,
breaks through multiplicitly and is transfixed by God, and
by the fact of his piercing me I pierce him in return: God
leads this spirit into the desert, into the solitude of its own
self, where it is simply one and is welling up in itself. This
spirit has no why, for if it had a why the unity would also
have its why. This spirit is in unity and freedom.

Meister Eckhart (1260–1327),
Sermons and Collations, LXXIV, 'The Promise of the Father'

CHAPTER THREE

Historical Crises:
From Incarnation to Imagination

Mystic experience is less time's enemy because, somehow, it stands outside history than because it discovers eternity in history's heart. By declaring limits time also extends opportunity, and through a consequent interplay of restriction and freedom the principle of Incarnation is to be grasped.

As we have seen, St Augustine's 'spiritual vision' teaches that the significance of God's book, the world, and of his Son, the Logos, is part of a process whereby saving truths become known to individuals through time. Augustine also speculates on a historical panorama involving Seven Ages of Man, whereby civilisation advances towards the eternal Jerusalem. During this process, Christ's Church labours against imperfection, its own and others', and agrees to call itself 'Militant'. For its comfort, the marching songs of Roman legions resounded with a new ideal along the ways of Empire, bearing the banner of a triumphal cross. Legions, however, they remained, and with all his fearless intensity, Augustine provided, to accompany his thrilling metaphors and symbols of spiritual combat, a theory of just war which, if divorced from the theology of intellectual vision, was likely to become an instrument of unjust, merely temporal powers.

Within Christianity as among other religions, however, theocentric saints especially have borne witness to the futility – and, ultimately, the injustice – of attempting to sustain one's self by things of time alone. Yet Christianity must take time seriously because God revealed himself in Jesus Christ at a certain historical moment. From that point of concentration, a confluence of Greek, Hebrew and Roman cultures permeated mediaeval learning and institutions, and then the new upheavals of Renais-

sance and Reformation which heralded the birth of a modern
empirical, as distinct from theological, science. Nevertheless,
and despite its novel emphasis on technological expertise, em-
piricism was powered still by an old ideal: that of bringing about
the same new heaven on a renewed earth as had energised the
Church Militant from the initiation. Theories maintaining that
the rise of science was a triumph of rationalism unshackling itself
from religious superstition are valid in only a restricted sense;
historians tell us also how deeply intertwined is the early history
of science with religious matters. Of course, a modern physicist
can profess non-Christian faith, or none at all, for with new
philosophy came secularism and the sensible acceptance of a right
to disbelief. But, for all the attainment of such freedom, the
circumstances in which science arose suggest, simply, that in its
history the history of Christianity remains implicit.[1]

The doctrine of Incarnation is especially pertinent to these
remarks, because incarnation can be described as the process by
which Spirit makes available to us the material world – through
the emergence, that is, in history, of a self-conscious and
responsible human Spirit from the Spirit of nature, so that man
comes to stand increasingly over and against, as well as in, his
material environment.[2] 'I and my Father are One' (John: 10, 30),
Jesus pronounced, knowing himself spiritual; and 'Why callest
thou me good?' (Matt: 19, 17), acknowledging his acceptance of
the limits of place and time, as a person who would die *in concreto*,
although the divine nature *in genere* would not.[3] Jesus, in short,
knew himself as a historical event in terms of which we may
come to grasp, though not fathom, the eternal mystery by which
Divinity is both separate from, and also within the world.
Reflecting the enigma, human consciousness finds itself,
similarly, in a predicament of detached agonist, and the variety of
syntheses which the human mind effects, imaginatively, to live
in this situation may be said to constitute the history of the
Incarnate Word. As Evelyn Underhill remarks, Incarnation is 'an
everlasting bringing forth in the universe and also in the
individual ascending soul, of the divine and perfect Life'.[4]

During the Middle Ages, literary expression of contemplative
experience by and large reflects a widespread but epistemologically unself-critical attitude to incarnation by assuming that
physical nature is a theophany 'in' and 'through' which God is
declared, and which language grasps. St Bonaventure's

Itinerarium Mentis in Deum, for example, declares that although degrees of knowledge prior to union are imperfect, traces of the mystery are within them, so that contemplative prayer and intellectual vision are, as it were, continuous with ordinary knowledge. St Bernard likewise recounts how his love of God has its first stirrings in carnal experience wherein the higher, spiritual state is intimated:

> To my thinking, this appears to have been one of the main reasons why the invisible God willed to appear in visible flesh, and as Man to converse amongst men, that, namely, He might draw all the affections of carnal men, who knew how to love only in a carnal manner, first to a salutory love of His own Flesh, and thence lead them gradually to a more spiritual love of his divinity.[5]

We can, legitimately, have a 'carnal love' of Jesus, although we pass beyond such devotion in union with God, who is pure Spirit. Bernard's stress on Incarnation assures us of mediation between God and Man, so that by the things of nature our gaze is turned effortlessly towards things of spirit.

Yet, as David Knowles reminds us, mysticism deals with God's approach to individual souls, so that in studying it we should expect to encounter the abnormal and anomalous.[6] Augustine after all had spoken savagely of how miserable and fragmented is the human condition as a result of the primal catastrophe, the Fall of Man. The Church on earth consequently has laboured amidst error's 'endless train', and even within the pale of orthodoxy a variety of types and notions – peculiar, world-hating, odd, licentious – have jostled continually. In all their wisdom, the Desert Fathers can strike us as acrid and peculiar: Abba Zeno was tempted, once, to eat a cucumber, 'So he rose and stood in the sun for five days, without drinking, and dried himself in the heat'. Still, some hermits lived, not in hatred of nature, but in special harmony with it, and in their very renunciation of a claim upon it, felt its true beauty: 'The Abba said: "Man is like a tree. . . . So we ought to take every precaution about guarding the mind, because that is our fruit. Yet we need to be covered and beautiful with leaves, the bodily discipline."'[7] In short, the theory of Augustine, or Bernard, or Bonaventure should not blind us to the variety of mediaeval experience, or to the similarity between that experience and our own.

Of course, the question is tricky: different civilisations *do* think and feel differently,[8] and literature has its imaginative life in enabling us to relive experiences of different cultural and psychological kinds, thereby mirroring the process of history's particular differences and perennial ordinariness. As far as contemplative life is concerned, monasticism was, during the Middle Ages, the major institutional means for catering to mystically inclined temperaments, enabling them in some conventional way to take up a perspective on the world, and, through the world, upon God. The intellectual basis for that possibility is recorded mainly in the writings of Augustine, Gregory, the Cistercians, Bernard and Bonaventure. Their teaching is at one with the sacral beauty of the liturgy, of the great cathedrals and the religious lyrics. It is, despite its acknowledgement of personal responsibility to God, remarkably free from stress on an individual's seeking, through a unique psychological makeup, a way to salvation distinct from the way of mankind as a whole.[9] The liturgy expresses no self-centred desire; its celebrant performs an appointed office, and if the priest is set apart it is because the holy ritual takes him as its instrument for representing God's action; not because, as an individual, he merits being set apart. Such practice has its dangers, certainly, and the office should not excuse the man's imperfections: *Ex ore tuo te judico, serve nequam*. The Bonaventuran 'in' and 'through' rather should irradiate a general Christian ideal, affirming that creatures exist for their functions (in man, to serve God freely) so that by way of a corporate striving the spiritual health of all together may be preserved enlivening that of each.

As a matter of history, this kind of approach to the spiritual life was fundamentally modified as soon as it became seriously a question whether human language *did* grasp the common nature inhering in things of the same species, or whether universals were confined to the mind alone. The term usually associated with a widespread tendency towards the latter view among philosophers and theologians of the fourteenth and fifteenth centuries is 'Nominalism'. But it is now the fashion to abjure the term, and recent scholarship is careful to circumscribe conclusions widely accepted a generation ago, which associated the movement with fideism, scepticism and destruction of the scholastic synthesis.[10] Nominalism, if we care to use the word at all, rather stands for a general tendency to restore to religion a fresh sense both of divine sovereignty and of God's immediacy in human experience.[11] It is less a doctrinal unity than a common attitude, and is not primarily based on a failure of nerve or desire to subvert.

William of Occam (c. 1300–50) speaks most prominently for the new tendency, and a key element in his thought deploys a well-worn distinction between God's absolute and ordained powers. His *absolute power*, the argument goes, cannot be estimated from things as they are, because God could have chosen other kinds of creation, and other schemes of salvation. His *ordained power*, by contrast, is what he has in fact willed and brought about.[12]

This distinction is crucial to William of Occam because, by using it to demonstrate the non-necessary nature of creation, he is able to stress that God in his absolute power is also the founder of a certain order of creation in which contingency itself demands special attention as a divinely appointed means of affecting man's salvation. The epistemological consequences of this theological stress on contingency are at once evident in Occam's special interest in perception, what he calls 'intuitive cognition'. We know individuals primarily; concepts are in the mind only ('in anima et verbo'), and are not essences shared by the thing with other members of the species.

It is easy, at this point, to underestimate Occam's complexity by concluding that universals must be, for him, subjective. To the contrary, he argues that there is a foundation for universals in nature, and so does not, in the end, break entirely with scholastic realism. But his drift is nonetheless clear: the mind's task lies in deciphering and processing linguistic realities which have an attentuated link with things, and which are, therefore, constantly in need of clarification and verification. For Occam, as for many of his contemporaries, mental images, simply, were in process of becoming divorced from concepts.

The development of Occam's kind of thought during the next century and into the period of Renaissance and Reformation is, like the history of all interesting ideas, complex. But its effect in one respect is certain: discontinuity between the mind's images and the archetypal Ideas to which created species were held to conform, became a premise of the new philosophy of nature which grew out of nominalism and into the scientific revolution.

Descartes stands at the parting of the ways. The realm of extension is real, he held, because its primary qualities are pre-eminently measurable. The mind stands opposed to extension, unhappily investing it sometimes with fanciful or analogical significance not inherent in the thing itself. Imagination must yield, therefore, to rational processes of measuring and weighing if laws governing matter are truly to be discovered.

Descartes, of course, kept his God, and also the scholastic language of his early education, though subsequent thinkers did their best to divest him of both. But God, the first cause, was now so emphatically transcendent that legitimate human knowledge was limited to secondary causes operating within our natural world. Two plus two, Descartes repeated, echoing the nominalists, could be, for God, something other than four. Such fideism on the one hand piously affirmed the divine omnipotence, and, in so doing guaranteed nature's order. On the other hand, however, it divorced the Great Originator from his book, the world – except, that is, in so far as we may come to appreciate an architectural structure which suggests a designer, now absent or remote.

Descartes retained also the scholastic doctrine of substances; a material substance, he held, underlies extension, as a spiritual substance underlies our thinking selves. Such stable forms at least could be relied upon to give us a secure perspective on ourselves and nature. Subsequent developments of Cartesian thought, however, especially in England, devoted much energy to divesting the theory of these mediaeval simplicities. First Locke, then Berkeley and Hume, stripped Descartes of his innate ideas and of his substances, first material, and then both material and spiritual. Hume at last admitted the world a queer place, but allowed us to assert no more, epistemologically, than a bare association of sense impressions. And Hume's most famous reader, Immanuel Kant, went on to conclude that we cannot know the world as it is in itself at all: the 'noumenal' eludes us. We must rest content with the 'phenomenal', that which we construct by perception, through artificial categories of space and time. For Kant, the old sense of man as a borderer, perpetually polarised by mystery, remains, but in a world where metaphysics is dead.

The new epistemology thus turned its back on an Augustinian approach to a God-centred continuity between language and things, images and ideas, and for literature of mysticism, the effect was dramatic.[13] The fourteenth century which gave rise to the nominalist debate, saw also a remarkable development of mystical writing, and the hallmark was now an individual voice, as of a person standing out from the corporate way to describe a particular experience, often with warmth and concreteness, and, sometimes, stridency. The author of the *Cloud of Unknowing*, for instance, indicates in his preface a clear consciousness of the potentially unsettling force of his words:

> I charge and beg you, with all the strength and power that love can bring to bear, that whoever you may be who possess this book (perhaps you own it, or are keeping it, carrying it, or borrowing it) you should, quite freely and of set purpose, neither read, write, or mention it to anyone, nor allow it to be read, written, or mentioned by anyone unless that person is in your judgement really and wholly determined to follow Christ perfectly. And to follow him not only in the active life, but to the utmost height of the contemplative life that is possible for a perfect soul in a mortal body to attain by the grace of God. And he should be, in your estimation, one who has for a long time been doing all that he can to come to the contemplative life by virtue of his active life. Otherwise the book will mean nothing to him.[14]

The book, in short, has an autonomous power to modify consciousness, and our genial author fears it. He no longer assumes that images displayed in a beautiful text can signify objective designs for the spirit's guidance. Words, rather, have attained a distinctive fickleness, a deceptiveness, a non-relation to things, and one feels here the characteristic ethos of that wider philosophical movement of the times, so intent on distinguishing between unique contingencies calling on us to act, and the entanglements of language through which we attempt to organise ourselves. The author of the *Cloud* clearly calls for right action, but he knows too that even the best-turned language bears a tenuous relation to the outside world, and can be construed wrongly if a reader has the will to do so.

Still, it would be difficult, doctrinally, to distinguish the fourteenth-century English mystics from Augustine, Bernard and Bonaventure: nor should we desire firm distinctions which

would distort genuine continuity. The relationship of nominalism to tradition is, after all, complex, and the effects of
nominalism on mysticism are subtle and indirect. They can,
however, for our present purposes be summed up in the
observation that Spirit's interior life is more acutely felt as
nature's objective significance is brought into question. Not
surprisingly, such a line of development stimulated fresh debate
on Incarnation, the doctrine which tells how Christ comes into
our everyday lives among material things, and how he is to be
detected there.

The most influential manual reflecting the new concern is *Of
the Imitation of Christ* (c. 1418). The author, Thomas à Kempis,
insists vigorously on the primacy of inner life, and is sceptical
about the values of rites and symbols if they are not accompanied
by the correct internal disposition. As a recent commentator
says:

> The notion of human character taken for granted by *The
> Imitation of Christ* is clearly very different from that of the
> medieval Church, outlined above. What it stresses is not the
> mystery of the Incarnation but the moral goodness of Christ
> the man; not his Passion and Resurrection, but his parables and
> teachings. The medieval Church did not talk about an *imitation*
> of Christ. Man, since he was made in God's image, was,
> essentially, already like Christ . . . . *The Imitation of Christ*, on
> the other hand, seems to take it for granted that man is essen-
> tially unlike Christ and that only through a studied conformity
> of the spirit will he find any salvation. Where the medieval
> Church saw man as a being in the process of realising himself,
> the *Imitation* is not interested in what he is but only in what he
> ought to be. The stress on *imitation* thus implies a loss of faith in
> the phenomenal world and a loss of belief in the idea that man
> is made in God's image. By advocating the imitation of Christ
> in this way the author implicitly dismisses the idea that there is
> something in man which is not only like Christ, but *is* Christ.
> As a result freedom and morality, outer and inner are set up in
> opposition to one another. It is the first symptom of a far-
> reaching change. [15]

Thomas à Kempis would perhaps be shocked to learn that he had
lost faith in the idea that man is made in God's image, but Gabriel

Josipovici's concluding oppositions are evident in the literature
he discusses, and the new high-strung introspection of Thomas à
Kempis is characteristic also of the efflorescence of mystical
literature in Europe at the end of the Middle Ages and during the
Renaissance, which reached fruition in the great literary achievements of St Teresa of Avila and St John of the Cross. In these two
figures especially, the life of contemplative prayer is examined
with unprecedented fullness and attention to its own implicit
nature, as a special state distinct from the life of ordinary prayer
and ordinary ways of knowing. In both, there is constant, in-
tensive suspicion of hallucinatory experiences and false imagin-
ings, and concern to describe and distinguish such works of the
devil from genuine vision. As is well known, St Teresa's writing
is full of practical good sense, humour and charm, but her main
aim is to describe a particular, individual progress to the heights,
through a series of extraordinary states of prayer. Her distinctions between phases of 'recollection' and 'quiet', 'spiritual
marriage' and 'union', document with a unique intensity of
introspective analysis, experiences which distinguish, and so
isolate, the mystic. Her beloved companion, St John, though
more theological and less autobiographical, complements her
achievement by charting the austere course of a spectacular
ascent of Mount Carmel through the dark nights of sense and
spirit, to the obscure brilliance of God's self-revelation, a journey
to which special souls, but not all, are sometimes called. St John
and St Teresa, clearly, do not write for all Christians equally, and
here the literature of mysticism reaches an extreme reflexive
stage, driven to locate its special quality in the individual's unique
psychological encounter with the divine, rather than to describe
the Way to God through an ascending scale mirrored in the
hierarchy of nature itself, which language truly denominates.[16]

The Cartesian dualism of Mind and Matter thus brings to a
head, much like Luther's dualism of faith and works, a tendency
long nurtured within late mediaeval Christendom, by which
Spirit declared its interiority. The scientific revolution, intensi-
fying nominalist thought, developed a correspondingly opposite
and intense interest in 'objective' nature, initiating a period, as
Carlyle says, of Victorious Analysis. Writers on the spiritual life
of course did not ignore challenges posed by the new science with
its attendant secularism, and this is especially clear in France,
where Descartes' influence on mystical writing was most

direct.[17]

Descartes' confessor was Pierre de Bérulle, founder of the French Oratorians, and later a cardinal whose special, papally-conferred title was 'Apostle of the Incarnate Word'. Bérulle was impressed by his young protegé, Descartes, and undertook to develop a mystical theology according to Cartesian principles. Bérulle consequently founded the so-called 'French school', and his encounter with scientific rationalism in the name of the Incarnate Word is a matter of fundamental significance for the history of mysticism in the West.

This complex story may be reduced without undue distortion to some crucial insights and choices of direction. First, Bérulle[18] saw the necessity of effecting a change in mystical theology commensurate with that which Descartes was effecting for philosophy. Consequently, Bérulle announced his own 'Copernican revolution'. He insisted on an uncompromising theocentricism, stressing everywhere the mystery of divine transcendence, and, with Descartes, acknowledging the futility of scholastic argument by analogy. It was for Bérulle's follower, Gibieuf, to make explicit in a systematic way the principle that God's transcendence implies God's superiority to causes which we observe at work in nature, and to reaffirm therefore the insignificance of science for approaching divine mysteries. But Gibieuf did not have to develop Bérulle very far in order to arrive at these conclusions.

Bérulle's theocentricism, however, is not entirely Cartesian, and he contrives to combine dualism with a traditional Augustinian insistence that self-mortification is the channel whereby divine grace works secretly in the soul to renovate natural knowledge. To explain this theory, Bérulle looks, like Thomas à Kempis, to the notion of imitating Christ. We are conformed to God in the degree to which it is open for our everyday lives to be Christlike, and this in each of us according to our particular vocations, gifts and aptitudes. These 'capacities' should be raised up in selfless adoration, until, at last, they become permanent dispositions. Bérulle acknowledges the importance of God's assuming material flesh, but Christ's actions in the body are, pre-eminently, exemplary. The physical (like the ego) must be stripped of appurtenances of naturalism in order to reveal the pure 'state' (*état*) of the soul's adherence to God, a purely spiritual knowledge.

Bérulle therefore accepts from the new thinkers that God's purposes are not well perceived in the images of material nature, though material nature must not be despised, because Christ assumed it. Bérulle asserts that divine mysteries are intuited, rather, by the mind's spiritual faculty, a process which depends on supernatural grace and not on the deliberate interrogation of natural images in the book of the world. How, then, we are to relate the physical world to the mind at all is a pressing question, and Bérulle does not face it directly.

Bérulle's predecessor and teacher, the Capucin Benet of Canfield,[19] had offered a solution to this question, based on psychology. Benet considered the world of extension useful for devotional purposes because things of nature seen in themselves are so repugnant to intellect and so frightening to the mind's eye, that we recoil from such a prospect to the comfort of spiritual sense. Literature written from this perspective tends, understandably, to be dramatic, and finds myriad expressions in devotional books throughout the baroque period. It is based not so much on polar synthesis as on polar opposition: as God assumed an immutable transcendence in proportion to the world's increasingly congealed inanity, the images of rhetoric hurtled in the midst of a great divide, and with desperate elation called attention to the dimensions of the gap that had to be jumped.

Nicolas Malebranche,[20] Bérulle's most famous successor, faced the 'Incarnational' problem philosophically, rather than psychologically as Benet had done. In the manner of Bérulle, Malebranche also desired to reconcile St Augustine with Descartes, and his thinking led him to the doctrine of Occasionalism. Briefly, he concluded that, because matter cannot modify spirit, the impingement of things upon our senses is the *occasion* for God's illumination of our minds, by way of a law of psychophysical parallelism which effects in us both sensation and ideas.

Malebranche's thought is elegant and has its special beauty. He knew that the 'hard' world of the rationalists and scientists must somehow be redeemed for God without surrendering the gains science was making. He knew, also, that man's control over nature must not encourage him to arrogate to himself, unduly, the powers of autonomous creation. For this reason, like Bérulle, Malebranche insisted (in contradiction of Descartes) that we have no clear idea of ourselves: all we know is 'in God', on whom our clear thoughts are wholly dependent. Malebranche therefore encourages the scientific assumption that there is a material world which we should investigate, and also insists that what scientists know is known in God, in the mysterious inner life of spirit. Knowledge 'in God' alone has the quality of self-evidence, while the world of bodies becomes an object of faith.

Malebranche's solution failed to take hold in European thought, and, especially at the hands of John Locke, was lifted up, shaken until the seams split, and more or less cast aside.[21] Locke's conclusions, which were to be wholeheartedly championed by the Enlightenment, rather supposed that the world of bodies was self-evident, so that God became the object of faith.

There is much, of course, to question in the curiously muddled commonsense of Locke's *Essay on Human Understanding*, but the broad conclusion remains that Locke stablised the divorce between Spirit and matter by moving exactly in the opposite direction to Malebranche. Both men wished for a certitude of clear ideas, distrusting imagination. But for one, clear ideas were a quasi-mystical knowledge 'in God'; for the other, they were perceptions of things.

The rise of science therefore presented a crisis for the literature of mysticism, precisely because it called into question the way in which the doctrine of Incarnation is to be understood. The process by which Spirit gives us, through our senses, the world of Matter is, as always, a mystery. In mediaeval tradition the theory of 'spiritual vision' suggested that words truly convey the divinely ordained species of things. But during the Renaissance and Enlightenment, when Spirit and Matter were defined more sharply in opposition, an intensified self-consciousness caused Spirit to stand, as it were, paralysed by a new sense of its own interior freedom faced with the vast and inert passivity of things which it must undertake to direct and invest with significance.

At this point, Locke can be seen both to anticipate the later development of Romanticism,[22] and to resist it. Despite his explicit, non-Romantic distrust of fictive imagination, Locke, by confining knowledge to perception and reflection – to the domain, that is, of image-making – laid the basis for a Romantic aesthetic theory concerned with the mind's mysterious interaction with nature. As M. H. Abrams points out, in Augustinian theology the major themes are God, natural creation and man; by contrast, although God is not altogether missing among the

Romantics, he is either given very little to do (as in Words-worth), or else identified with the process of nature itself.[23] 'God,' as Schelling's disciple, the naturalist Oken, says, 'is a man representing God in self-consciousness.'[24] From here, it is but a short step to Darwin, who, concentrating on the material facts, suggested a hypothesis in which fitness for survival replaced Providence, and from which God was, at last, conspicuously absent.

Although most Romantic thought stops short of Darwin and retains, however implicitly, the mystery of incarnation and other traditional *topoi* in the Christian scheme of salvation, these elements tend to undergo a general displacement, as Abrams says, from a 'supernatural to a natural frame of reference' (p. 13). Wordsworth, for instance, no less than Milton, is concerned to restore man to an earthly paradise, but does so by way of a strangely novel 'secular theodicy – a theodicy without an operative *theos*' (p. 95), whereby salvation is attained within 'the world/ Of all of us, the place in which, in the end,/ We find our happiness, or not at all' (*Prelude* III, 194). Even in Blake, who saw Wordsworth as far too pagan, and whose own interest in Jehovah was well marked, the drama of salvation is typically Romanti-cised, so that Jesus, in whom the mystery of incarnation pre-eminently resides, is explicitly identified with imagination: 'Imagination . . . is the Divine Body of the Lord Jesus, blessed for ever' (*Jerusalem*, 5, 58–9).

The Romantic revolution thus poses special questions for the history of mysticism because it develops to the end term a tendency implicit in nominalism, and at last turns the old Neo-Platonist, Augustinian scheme upside down. The dominant emphasis, that is, has shifted away from a 'uniformitarian' Absolute, divine guarantor of nature's order and stability, to a 'diversitarian', radically evolutionist conception of deity.[25] The resultant temper and mood of religious feeling were distinctive and momentous, proposing the possibility – even the necessity – of religion without transcendence.

The approximation of a mediaeval doctrine of Incarnation to a Romantic theory of imagination is, therefore, it should now appear, less a rejection of traditional faith than a reassurance that we are divinely blessed, as ever, in mind's mysterious union with nature; still involved, that is, with the process in which spirit gives us the material world. Moreover, we are free to have our particular, individualised brands of religion, a state of affairs which, Schleiermacher suggests, it is the special distinction of Christianity to bring about.[26] We are at liberty, in short, to become the visionaries of our own ideals, saints of our own cult, prophets of our own distinctiveness. At best, such diversity cultivates toleration, a genuine appreciation of the right of others to be different and to believe different things. At worst, it breeds egotism, and 'especially – in the political and social sphere – of the kind of collective vanity which is nationalism or racialism'.[27]

In such a situation, faced on one hand with the disenchanted nature of positivists and Darwinians, and on the other with a widespread tendency to view religious experience as mainly psychological, expression of the age-old mystic claim to an objective encounter with the Absolute and transcendent God meets with special and acute difficulties. For how does such a claim distinguish itself from the merely subjective or fictional; where in the world does it discover the marks of transcendence without merely displaying nostalgia for transcendence lost; how can it face the facts and, also, speak persuasively? In a sense, these kinds of questions have always challenged the mystics, but in the nineteenth century they produce, among the best writers, a characteristic format: that of 'nature mysticism' resonant also with the peculiarly modern anguish of *Deus Absconditus*.

The Victorian Richard Jefferies (1848–87)[28] provides a striking example of this combination of effects because he knew nature with a Romantic sensibility akin to Wordsworth's, and, also, he had read and well understood the disenchanting message of Darwin. His writings are thus well-suited to showing how a historical assimilation of Incarnation to imagination provokes the most radical theological questions; but also how, despite historical circumstances, the mystic's intuitions are still comparable to those of writers for whom traditional faith might seem to have been more obvious, and somehow, easier.

In a variety of literary forms, including letters, newspaper and journal articles, novels, pamphlets, country books and romances, Richard Jefferies has left a surprisingly abundant witness, considering his short life, to the state of English rural society during a period when industrialisation and agricultural depression were fast destroying such country traditions as had survived enclosure and the progressive conversion of farming to corporate business interests. Also, driven by a kind of positivist consciousness and moral fervour, Jefferies had early rejected the tenets of orthodox religion as superstitions serving only to blinker and confine the mind. 'Deity and the whole range of superstition', he writes in a notebook, 'invented because of misery':[29]

> How can I adequately express my contempt for the assertion that all things occur for the best, for a wise and beneficent end, and are ordered by a humane intelligence! It is the most utter falsehood and a crime against the human race . . . . There is not the least trace of directing intelligence in human affairs.[30]

'There is', he concludes, 'no consolation' (p. 182); yet, out of this very conclusion he is prepared to declare hope.

The tension between Jefferies' visionary intuition of the 'real state' of what he calls 'soul life' arising from his solitary meditations on nature, and the clear-headed, unsentimental modern observer of men and society, is evident throughout *The Story of My Heart*, the book Jefferies calls 'a confession' (p. x), 'absolutely and unflinchingly true' (p. viii), and which has been described as the 'central document'[31] among the author's works. Jefferies' own summary is worth quoting:

> This book is a confession. The Author describes the successive stages of emotion and thought through which he passed, till he arrived at the conclusions which are set forth in the latter part of the volume. He claims to have erased from his mind the traditions and learning of the past ages, and to stand face to face with nature and with the unknown. The general aim of the work is to free thought from every trammel, with the view of its entering upon another and larger series of ideas than those which have occupied the brain of man so many centuries. He believes that there is a whole world of ideas outside and beyond those which now exercise us. (pp. x–xi)

The description, which Jefferies felt inadequate, is a fair, if limited, indication of one of the book's main lines of argument. But in the body of his writing Jefferies tries to catch the process itself of setting thought free, and of entering into his 'larger series of ideas'. For instance, he alludes repeatedly to the figure of a circle: if the circumference expands, so does thought, but if it stays fixed, the circle is an imprisoning enclosure, like 'the revolution of a wheel' (p. 195) with fixed spokes, a merely mechanical effect. To this imprisoning circle, Jefferies likens the tedious superficial round of city life, and the limited circle of ideas that descends from tradition to destroy independence of mind. But there are also 'whole circles of ideas unknown to us' (p. 169) and instead of working 'round and round inside the circle' (p. 54) thought needs continually to develop outwards.

Most often Jefferies alludes directly to circles when he intends us to see them as restricting: the sense for instance, in which 'our ideas have run in circles for centuries' (p. 144). 'The mind', he writes, 'or circle, or sequence of ideas, acts, or thinks, or exists in a balance, or what seems a balance to it' (p. 142). This 'balanced' circle suggests a watch, symbolising mechanical order. It is akin to the enclosure of a husk (p. 2), in turn associated with a pall of dust (p. 1), just as the interminable round of tramping feet in London is like a grinding wheel.

On the other hand, the circle is 'like a hyperbola that continually widens ascending' (p. 181), and at best, Jefferies' prose captures a breathless, swelling sense of expansiveness, as the mind, through nature, discovers the glorious mystery of its own existence. Within a 'perfect amphitheatre' of hills, for example, the circle of sun expands a single flower into the encompassing circular petal of sky (pp. 4–5), as the music of the author's soul 'swelled forth' (p. 6) through the 'earth-encircling air' (p. 6). Unlike the horse tethered to a stake (p. 107), the mind grows (p. 54) through nature's rhythms, progressive as the 'swell of the cycles' (p. 19) of a tide, reaching ever further 'onwards into an ever-widening ocean of idea and life' (p. 204). The visionary gleam finds expression through a communion with things in openness which the expanding circle represents, as a kind of dialogue which Jefferies calls 'prayer':

> I spoke it with the ear of wheat as the sun tinted it golden; with the whitening barley; again with the red gold spots of autumn on the beech, the buff oak leaves, and the gossamer dew-weighted. All the larks over the green corn sang it for me, all the dear swallows; the green leaves rustled it; the green brook-flags waved it; the swallows took it with them to repeat it for me in distant lands. (p. 22)

There is, however, anguish in Jefferies' *Story* and we can best get at it by looking at his circles in the negative sense suggested by the equation of watch-face to nature's blind mechanism. Jefferies everywhere insists that nature's laws, although consistent and mechanically structured, show no evidence of guiding intelligence, and are in no way designed to assist or illuminate humanity but rather to confine it. Jefferies knew his Darwin, and is remorselessly opposed to the glib consolations of the world's Paleys, that nature's design entails a beneficent designer. Nature is 'a force without a mind' (p. 71), and 'no deity has anything to do with nature' (p. 70). Nature is non-teleological, and is governed by chance and the economy of force: it is indifferent to man, even 'anti-human' (p. 64). In face of this, and of the sufferings to which flesh is heir, there is 'no consolation. There is no relief' (p. 182). Jefferies is unyielding on the point, and his explicit refusal to find any 'traces' whatsoever of deity in nature shows how far, in this respect, he differs from the medieval saints.

How, then, are we to see Jefferies as part of a tradition of Western mysticism at all? A place to begin is his dissatisfaction with Darwin, despite his thoroughly Darwinian view of nature's blind and savage energies. 'There is no evolution any more than there is any design in nature' (p. 137), he writes, perplexingly. And, in a notebook: 'Natural selection a true cause, modifying, but not a sufficient cause to explain all phenomena'.[32]

Darwin himself, of course, had not claimed that his hypothesis explained everything, and was careful to say so, repeatedly. He had, however, shown no real concern (nor should we expect him to) with those aspects of human experience on which natural selection had no bearing. Here is a passsage from *Origin of Species* in which Darwin discusses his key term:

> In the literal sense of the word, no doubt, natural selection is a false term; but who ever objected to chemists speaking of the elective affinities of the various elements? – and yet an acid cannot strictly be said to elect the base with which it in preference combines. It has been said that I speak of natural selection as an active power or Deity; but who objects to an author speaking of the attraction of gravity as ruling the movements of the planets? Every one knows what is meant and is implied by such metaphorical expressions; and they are

almost necessary for brevity. So again it is difficult to avoid personifying the word Nature; but I mean by Nature, only the aggregate action and product of many natural laws, and by laws the sequence of events as ascertained by us. With a little familiarity such superficial objections will be forgotten.[33]

'Metaphorical' and 'superficial' are the telling words, and mark a main line of division between Darwin and Jefferies, who could not at all see that the mind's contribution, through metaphor, was a matter of surfaces: Jefferies saw force as the really superficial thing, and mind's activity as the deep and worthwhile aspect of experience. Indeed, the word 'deep' is used with remarkable frequency throughout *The Story of My Heart*,[34] and Jefferies' sense of wonder is consistently associated with the third dimension which it suggests. Matter, by contrast, as we have seen, is a wheel, a clock-face, and the shallow routine of those trapped by civilisation and convention. Interestingly, Jefferies on two occasions tells us he is no lover of paintings, because the flat surfaces seem dead to him (pp. 26, 88): he prefers sculpture. A reason for this relatively unexplained aesthetic taste perhaps comes through his equation, elsewhere, of surfaces to mechanism, and the third dimension (shared by sculpture) with the 'depth' of inner life, the power of psyche, discoverer of form (pp. 24–5). Partly *because* of his Darwinian disenchantment, therefore, Jefferies is *especially* fascinated with the incarnational mystery: the fact that an alien, mindless material universe enables psyche to discover and come to know its own 'interior' powers.

And yet the moral problem remains. God cannot be permitted into our universe because explanations which refer evil and suffering to divine purpose are 'a crime against the human race' (p. 146). In a terrible passage, Jefferies begins to consider the suffering of children, but leaves off ('I can hardly write of it' [p. 147]), explaining how he could not enter a hospital lest his mind be overcome (p. 147). There is something here, again, remarkably close to Darwin, whose career turned away from medicine because he could not bear to deal directly with suffering. Throughout his life and writings, Darwin remained extraordinarily sensitive to, and grieved by, the fact of pain, both animal and human. Like Jefferies, he could not admit a 'trace' of God in the affairs of nature, and explanations that eliminated from the world a morally unendurable Deity were, in a way, liberating. Except, of course, that unlike Darwin, Jefferies was afflicted by the exigency of his own 'soul life': without consolation, without relief, he allowed himself in the end to hope that beyond thought, beyond the circles of our present intuitions and dreams, there is something 'higher than deity' (p. 57). This unspeakable God is described no further, but simply attested from the depths of soul's experience, through soul's demand for 'something better than a god' (p. 184).

It is has become usual to classify Jefferies as a 'nature mystic': one whose vision is intense, but whose range (or depth) is limited.[35] Such a diagnosis seems fair, for *The Story of My Heart* is in many ways incomplete. Jefferies tells us he had meditated on the book for twelve years (p. vii) before writing it, but, despite the length of gestation, the result strikes one as unresolved, and part of the failure is intellectual.[36] One reason is that Jefferies' desire to be rid entirely and immediately of all that he calls 'tradition' leaves him without resources for explaining the intermediate steps between our present state and the perfect health and physical beauty which he desires for all people along with the defeat of disease, increase in leisure, and ability to face death without fear. The *process*, in short, of Jefferies' circles of expansion towards human happiness and towards the God beyond hope and consolation, is left out of account.

The Story of My Heart nonetheless remains a poetic document revealing through elegant prose, and in a display of the patterning processes of imagination, the reality of spirit: 'Analyse away the soul: the soul returns'.[37] But as a vision to live by, it remains less than satisfactory because, we might say, in dealing with Incarnation, Jefferies celebrates the inwardness of spirit through imagination at the expense of history and theology.

I have treated *The Story of My Heart* as symptomatic, therefore, because it raises questions central to the literature of mysticism in an age of science, and in a context of Romanticism. But Jefferies' sensibility is also of our own times, and he sounds surprisingly like certain modern radical theologians who also proclaim the death of a traditional God. 'I hope God will be forgiven',[38] Jefferies writes, and calls to mind a similar 'protest atheism' widespread in this century. 'A person who is fully a man of our times', writes John A. T. Robinson, the so-called 'atheist bishop', '*must* – or, at any rate, *may* – be an atheist before he can be a Christian.' Robinson is echoed by such as William Hamilton ('the death of God must be affirmed') or Gabriel Vahanian ('God is man's failure') and by numerous others. Admittedly, such provocative theology often ends by being less radical than it sounds: God is needed after all, these writers seem to mean, though we must beware of idolatries and criminal follies which the sentimentalists and soft-minded through the ages have associated with his name. As Simone Weil says: 'There are two atheisms of which one is a purification of the notion of God'. This is not far removed from what Vahanian and Hamilton really mean, or from Jefferies' denunciation of God in the name of 'something higher than deity'.[39]

If God has never been easy, the present age clearly has not made him any more so, and in this context, Richard Jefferies is not just to be labelled a 'nature mystic'. He struggles, rather, to open his vision to transcendence without surrendering the challenges posed to him by *deus otiosus*, by suffering, and the fragmentation of tradition. No doubt the present age will have a fuller story to tell about the life of the spirit than is contained in the story of Jefferies' heart, but it will not ignore the questions Jefferies raises, or the struggles and intuitions which his writings record.

To summarise: Incarnation presents the mystery of transcendence and immanence to the minds and hearts of Western mystics according to a certain mode, which their literature reflects. The development of science intensifies, without radically altering, the challenges Incarnation poses to understanding; naturalism alone does not account for the structure and fact of knowledge or the nature of universals, because natural science remains non-natural in its process, if not in the objects of its study. Some means, therefore, of preserving intact the old 'spiritual vision' amidst a new reign of quantity and spiritual inwardness becomes imperative. Imagination, having come to realise itself as a means of vision, contributes to this task, though imagination unaided does not discover how to explain itself as a means of grace. To re-experience incarnational mystery with its corporeal aspect in just relationship to the aspect that deals with ideas remains therefore a challenge to the separated domains of theologians, scientists and poets in our own time. Its solution perhaps does not lie, first, in each attempting to acquire the other's expertise, but in discovering how each may speak most fully, given what he knows, about being human within time's limits, through time's opportunity.

TEXTS WITHOUT COMMENT

3 FROM INCARNATION TO IMAGINATION

INCARNATION AND IMITATION

1. The beginning of Christendom is, strictly, at a point out of time. A metaphysical trigonometry finds it among the spiritual Secrets, at the meeting of two heavenward lines, one drawn from Bethany along the Ascent of Messias, the other from Jerusalem against the Descent of the Paraclete. That measurement, the measurement of eternity in operation, of the bright cloud and the rushing wind, is, in effect, theology.

   The history of Christendom is the history of an operation. It is an operation of the Holy Ghost towards Christ, under the conditions of our humanity; and it was our humanity which gave the signal, as it were, for that operation. The visible beginning of the Church is at Pentecost, but that is only a result of its actual beginning – and ending – in heaven. In fact, all the external world, as we know it, is always a result. Our causes are concealed, and mankind becomes to us a mass of contending unrelated effects. It is the effort to relate the effects conveniently without touching, without (often) understanding, the causes that makes life difficult. The Church is, on its own showing, the exhibition and the correction of all causes. It began its career by arguing about its own cause – in such time as it had to spare from its even greater business of coming into existence.

   Charles Williams (1886–1945),
Descent of the Dove, 1

2. For Thy concept is a Son, in whom are all things, and Thine union and Thy concept is act and operation arising therefrom – the act and operation wherein existeth the actuality and unfolding of all things. As therefore of Thee, the loving God, there is begotten the loveable God, and this generation is a concept, even so there proceedeth from Thee, the loving God, and from Thy concept, the loveable God begotten of Thee, Thine act and concept, to wit, the

bond knitting together and the God uniting Thee and Thy concept, even as the act of loving uniteth in love the lover and the beloved. And this bond is called Spirit; for spirit is like motion, proceeding from that which moveth and that which is moved. Thus motion is the unfolding of the concept of him that moveth. Wherefore in Thee, God the Holy Spirit, all things are unfolded, even as they are conceived in Thee, God the Son.

Nicholas of Cusa (1401–64),
The Vision of God, XIX

3. What a marvel it is that she should have laid her Creator and her God in her bosom; loving Him intensely above all imagining; and yet that she should never have doubted, but was always certain, that He was her God. She could behave to Him as His Mother, and He walked with her as her Child; and yet, never for one moment in all her life was she content with this; but in mind she soared ever above, and was lost in the Divine Abyss, in which alone she found her rest, her inheritance and her dwelling-place.

John Tauler (c. 1300–61), Sermon,
'On the Assumption of Our Lady'

4. The Father by loving became feminine: and the great proof of this is He whom He begot of Himself; and the fruit brought forth by love is love.

Clement of Alexandria (c. 160–220),
Salvation of the Rich Man, XXXVII

5. And though our earthly mother may suffer her child to perish, our heavenly Mother, Jesus, may not suffer us that are His children to perish: for He is All-mighty, All-wisdom, and All-love.

Julian of Norwich (1343–after 1413),
Revelations, 'Anent certain points', LXI

6. The longing to love the beauty of the world in a human being is essentially the longing for the Incarnation. It is mistaken if it thinks it is anything else. The Incarnation alone can satisfy it. It is therefore wrong to reproach the mystics, as has been done sometimes, because they use love's language. It is theirs by right. Others only borrow it.

Simone Weil (1909–43),
Waiting for God, 171–2

7. Do you observe how even Majesty must yield to love? So it

is, my brethren. Love can no more look up to, than it can
look down upon, any one. It allows of no distinction between lovers who truly love, but ever brings high and low
to an equality in itself. Indeed, not alone does it make them
equal, but it even makes them one. Perhaps you have
imagined that God is to be excepted from this law of love?
But the Apostle tells you that 'he who is joined to the Lord is
one spirit'. Why should we be surprised at this, since He has
made Himself as one of ourselves? I have not said enough.
For He has made Himself not merely as one, but really one
of ourselves. He is truly Man.

> Bernard of Clairvaux (1091–1153),
> *Sermons on the Canticles*, LIX

8. A good Man is One Spirit with Christ. Thus he is like
Christ, a Spirit of Universal Sweetness, which longs, and
labours to bring forth itself in Peace, and Pleasures every
where. When it meets with a Soul shut up in Griefs, it is
straitned and afflicted there, and burns like a Fire, to be at
liberty in that Heart. This Spirit suffers with each Heart, till
it can make every Heart to rejoyce with itself. It is never
entirely Risen from the Dead, while there is any one in the
Grave of Sorrows. That One is Member of its Body; and it is
ever present with the whole Body, being all of itself in every
Part of that; all in the Sorrows of the Militant and Suffering
Part, as truly as it is all in the Joys of the Triumphant, and
Rejoycing Part.

> Peter Sterry (c. 1614–72),
> *The Rise, Race and Royalty of the Kingdom
> of God in the Soul of Man*, 170

9. Love your enemies and do good to them that hate you, pray
for those that pursue you. And therefore if thou wilt follow
Christ be like to Him in this craft. Learn to love thine
enemies and sinful men, for all these are thine even-
Christians. Look and bethink thee how Christ loved Judas,
which was both His deadly enemy and a sinful caitiff.

> Walter Hilton (–1396),
> *Scale of Perfection*, I, 70

10. And then I saw that each kind compassion that man hath on
his even-Christians with charity, it is Christ in him.

> Julian of Norwich (1343–after 1413),
> *Revelations*, XIII, 28

11. The people, devotees of pleasure, strove after riches to their ruin; he willed to be poor. They longed for honors and power; he refused to be king. They considered sons according to the flesh a great blessing; he spurned such wedlock and offspring. They were extremely proud and dreaded reproach; he endured every kind of insult. They thought injuries to be intolerable; what injury could be greater than that a just, innocent man be condemned? They cursed bodily pain; he was scourged and tortured. They feared death; he was punished with death. They thought the cross an ignominious kind of death; he was crucified. All the things we desired to have when we did not live right he showed to be of no value by doing without them. All that we wished to avoid and which caused us to turn away from zeal for godliness, he bore patiently and made powerless. No sin can be committed which does not involve seeking after what he despised or fleeing from what he endured. Thus his whole life on earth, through the humanity which he condescended to assume, was an instruction in living righteously.

> William of St Thierry (1058–1148),
> *Enigma of Faith*, 12

12. And although the Humanity of Christ be the most holy and perfect means of access to God, the chief instrument of our salvation, and the channel, through which we receive every blessing for which we hope, nevertheless His Humanity is not the supreme good, for that consists in seeing God.

> Miguel de Molinos (1640–97),
> *The Spiritual Guide which Disentangles
> the Soul, Second Admonition*, 12

THE IMAGE OF GOD

13. As long as Jesus findeth not His image reformed in thee, He is strange and far from thee. Shape thee, therefore, to be arrayed in His likeness, that is in meekness and charity, the which are His liveries, and then will He homely know thee and show to thee His privities.

> Water Hilton (–1396),
> *Scale of perfection*, I, 51

14. In all faces is seen the Face of faces, veiled, and in a riddle; howbeit unveiled it is not seen, until above all faces a man enter into a certain secret and mystic silence where there is no knowldge or concept of a face. This mist, cloud, darkness or ignorance into which he that seeketh Thy face entereth when he goeth beyond all knowledge or concept, is the state below which Thy face cannot be found except veiled; but that very darkness revealeth Thy face to be there, beyond all veils. 'Tis as when our eye seeketh to look on the light of the sun which is its face; first it beholdeth it veiled in the stars, and in colours and in all things that share its light. But when it striveth to behold the light unveiled, it goeth beyond all visible light, because all this is less than that which it seeketh.

Nicholas of Cusa (1401–64),
The Vision of God, VI

15. Then there comes true and is realized the claim I have put forward in this little book, namely, that the good man, so far as he is good, takes on all the character of that same goodness which God is in himself.

Meister Eckhart (1260–1327),
The Book of Benedictus, I, 2

16. Consider how easy it is for the human soul at any time to reproduce the shape of any kind of thing in the imagination and to make any kind of original creature, as often as he wills, independent of pre-existing matter and as it were, from nothing. And so that which had seemed incredible at first will begin to be less marvellous. Wherein you will also begin to discover this very remarkable thing, namely that God who is the supreme truth, has reserved to himself the truth of things, but has conceded to his image the power of forming images of things at any time.

Richard of St Victor (–c. 1173),
Benjamin Major, IV, 20

17. To scorn the multitude of the city, is to avoid the evil employments of human conversation, so as no longer to take pleasure in imitating the abandoned manners of earthly men, who, through the abundance of iniquity, are many. For they desire to enter, with the few, the narrow gate, and seek not, with the many, to enter the broad roads which lead to destruction. For they carefully behold by Whom, and for

what, they are created; and from a right consideration of the image they have received, they disdain to follow the vulgar herd. Whence it is said by the voice of the Bridegroom to the Bride, in the Song of Songs, If thou knowest not thyself, O beautiful among women, go forth, and go thy way after the footsteps of the flocks, and feed thy kids. For she who is beautiful among women knows herself, when every Elect soul, though placed amongst sinners, remembers that it was fashioned after the image and similitude of its Creator, and goes on, in accordance with the similitude it has perceived.

Gregory the Great (540–604),
Morals on the Book of Job, Bk. xxx, 56

8. Nothing can be compared to the great beauty and capabilities of a soul; however keen our intellects may be, they are as unable to comprehend them as to comprehend God, for, as He has told us, He created us in His own image and likeness. As this is so, we need not tire ourselves by trying to realise all the beauty of this castle, although, being His creature, there is all the difference between the soul and God that there is between the creature and the Creator; the fact that it is made in God's image teaches us how great are its dignity and loveliness. It is no small misfortune and disgrace that, through our own fault, we neither understand our nature nor our origin.

Teresa of Avila (1515–82),
Interior Castle, First Mansion, I, 2–3

FREEDOM

19. Rather in fear and trembling work out your own salvation. Consider not what other men are, but, so far as in you lieth, what through you they may become; not those only that live now but also those who hereafter shall be born and whom ye shall have for followers in your holy intent.

William of St Thierry (1085–1148),
Golden Epistle, 3, 7

20. For a good will in the soul is the fountain of all good things and mother of all virtues. So on the contrariwise an evil will is the fountain of all evils and vices. Therefore the keeper of his soul ought to be very careful concerning the keeping of

his will, that he may wisely understand and discern that which he willeth wholly, or which he ought to will wholly, as the love of God; and that which he ought to will because of that, as the love of his neighbour.

William of St Thierry (1085–1148),
Golden Epistle, 15, 54

21. In like manner we ought not to speak of grace at such length and so vehemently as to give rise to that poisonous teaching which takes away free-will. Accordingly, we may speak of faith and grace, so far as we can with the help of God, for the greater praise of His divine Majesty, but not in such a way, especially in these dangerous times of ours, that works and free-will shall receive any detriment, or come to be accounted for nothing.

Ignatius Loyola (1491–1556),
Spiritual Exercises, 'Rules for Thinking
with the Church', XVII

22. That which is free, none may call his own, and he who maketh it his own, committeth a wrong. Now, in the whole realm of freedom, nothing is so free as the will, and he who maketh it his own, and suffereth it not to remain in its excellent freedom, and free nobility, and in its free exercise, doeth a grievous wrong.

Theologia Germanica (c. 1350), ch. LI

23. Lord! my feet are dappled by the blood of Thy Redemption, my wings are smooth because Thou hast nobly chosen me, my mouth is ordered by Thy Holy Spirit, mine eyes illumined by Thy fiery Light; my head composed because of Thy faithful protection; my flight hastened by Thy unresting care; my sinking to earth comes from Thy union with my body; the greater release Thou givest me from earthly things, the longer must I soar in Thee!

Mechthild of Magdeburg (1212–99),
Revelations, Part 2, 18

24. In the state of abandonment the only rule is the duty of the present moment. In this the soul is light as a feather, liquid as water, simple as a child, active as a ball in receiving and following all the inspirations of grace. Such souls have no more consistence and rigidity than molten metal. As this takes any form according to the mould into which it is poured, so these souls are pliant and easily receptive of any

form that God chooses to give them. In a word, their disposition resembles the atmosphere, which is affected by every breeze; or water, which flows into any shaped vessel exactly filling every crevice. They are before God like a perfectly woven fabric with a clear surface; and neither think, nor seek to know what God will be pleased to trace thereon, because they have confidence in Him, they abandon themselves to Him, and, entirely absorbed by their duty, they think not of themselves, nor of what may be necessary for them, nor of how to obtain it. The more assiduously do they apply themselves to their little work, so simple, so hidden, so secret, and outwardly contemptible, the more does God embroider and embellish it with brilliant colours.

Jean-Pierre de Caussade (1675–1751),
Abandonment to Divine Providence, I, ii, 12

25. O Adorable and Eternal GOD! hast thou made me a free Agent! And enabled me if I pleas to offend Thee infinitly! What other End couldst Thou intend by this, but that I might pleas Thee infinitly! That having the Power of Pleasing or displeasing I might be the friend of God! Of all Exaltations in all Worlds this is the Greatest. To make a World for me was much, to command Angels and Men to lov me was much, to prepare Eternall Joys for me was more. But to giv me a Power to displeas thee, or to set a Sin before Thy face, which Thou infinitly hatest, to profane Eternity, or to defile thy Works, is more stupendious then all these.

Thomas Traherne (1637–74),
Centuries, IV, 43

26. The Will, whether in God, or the Creature, is the Ground and Seed of every Thing; is the generating working Power, which maketh and worketh all Things to be in that State and Condition which they are; and that every Thing begins, goes on, and ends, in the Working of the Will; and that nothing can be otherwise, than as its Will worketh; and therefore Eternity and Time are magical; and Magic is, and must be, the Mother of all Things. Now here you see, in the utmost Degree of Clearness, how all true and false Religion divide from one another. For if nothing worketh but the Will, if nothing else carries on the Work of Nature, then all is false and vain in Religion, but the Working of the Will; and nothing is saving, or redeeming the Life of the Soul, but that

which helps the Will to work towards God.

William Law (1686–1761),

The Way to Divine Knowledge, Dialogue 2

27. God lies in wait for us therefore with nothing so much as
with love. For love is like the fisherman's hook. To the
fisherman falls no fish that is not caught on his hook. Once it
takes the hook the fish is forfeit to the fisherman; in vain it
twists hither and thither, the fisherman is certain of his
catch. And so I say of love: he who is caught thereby has the
strongest of all bonds and yet a pleasant burden. He who
bears this sweet burden fares further, gets nearer therewith
than by using any harshness possible to man. Moreover, he
can cheerfully put up with whatever befalls, cheerfully
suffer what God inflicts. Naught makes thee so much God
nor God so much thine own as this sweet bond. He who has
found this way will seek no other. He who hangs on this
hook is so fast caught that foot and hand, mouth, eyes and
heart and all that is man's is bound to be God's.

So then thou canst not, better than by love, prevail over
thy foe and stop him doing thee a mischief. Wherefore it is
written: 'Love is strong as death and hard as hell'. Death
separates soul from body, but love separates all things from
the soul; she will not tolerate at any cost what is not God nor
God's. Who is caught in this net, who walks in this way,
whatsoever he works is wrought by love, whose alone the
work is: busy or idle it matters nothing. Such an one's most
trivial action is more profitable, his meanest occupation is
more fruitful to himself and other people and to God is
better pleasing than the cumulative works of other men,
who, though free from mortal sin, are yet inferior to him in
love. He rests more usefully than others labour.

Await thou therefore this hook, so thou be happily
caught, and the more surely caught so much the more surely
freed.

That we may be thus caught and freed, help us O thou
who art love itself. Amen.

Meister Eckhart (1260–1327),

Sermons and Collations, IV,

'The Eternal Birth'

CHAPTER FOUR
Self and Ego

'Know Thyself': the oracle speaks in a riddle about a riddle.
Could we know ourselves completely, however, we would cease
to live in a human world where thinking emerges tentatively,
needing to be confronted and confirmed by others. Of course,
the oracle does not speak about knowing ourselves, or anything
else, *completely*. There is a riddle, and a promise, because the
statement makes a certain amount of sense, but not complete
sense. 'Know Thyself' seems to mean, also, 'acknowledge what
you can't know', which is the way Socrates seems to have taken
it. And St Paul understood that we cannot compel the saving
insight – that by which we may come to know ourselves as we
are known (1 Cor.: 13, 12) – by any amount of self-scrutiny.

The very idea of self-knowledge under examination therefore
soon confounds the irreducibly obvious in absurdity, a predicament which, properly understood, should curtail our overhasty
optimism on the one hand, or self-indulgent dejection on the
other. We know ourselves with maddeningly obscure simplicity, a fact to which we can attend, or refuse attention. The interrogation merely turns on itself, yielding nothing except its own
irresolvable presence, and finding terms to describe the mind's
position poised, thus, within an enigma not of its own invention,
is a delicate matter. It calls for subtlety (the issues being, like the
oracle, elusive), and for arbitrariness (as introspection chooses a
place to begin). And it brings us to the terms, 'ego' and 'self'.

To the degree that consciousness is separate from its object we
can say it is the seat of ego, centre of awareness in so far as 'I'
appears to itself to have identity and continuity. Through ego-
consciousness 'I' establishes itself as an individual, and as such
discovers responsibility, so that in ego lies also the ground of
moral awareness.

For a whole time's way of thinking, Freud has corrected beyond dispute a tendency to align mind with ego alone: the body's unconscious presence affects personality, and the bodily rootedness of mental images is a fact of radical importance for psychologists and moralists alike. But the body, thus conceived, it seems must also be an image, or incomplete representation of that human being which we never succeed in fully objectifying. Ego, after all, is conscious not just of its physical vehicle full of pains and alarms that do not originate with ego. The mind is also visited by a variety of self-surprising movements (an impulse, say, to jump out of that window, to dislike or love this person on first sight) and from the domain between body's unconscious processes and ego–consciousness, human creativity especially draws life. In that single 'throb of an artery'[1] which Yeats describes, the inspired poetic image makes manifest a creative unconscious for which physical mechanism does not fully account, and which envelops ego, as the whole contains one of its parts.

Raised upon Freud's foundations, Jung's thought has to do especially with the role of the unconscious in human creative activity, and, in this context, Jung distinguishes 'self' from 'ego': 'The self is a quantity that is superordinate to the conscious ego. It embraces not only the conscious but also the unconscious psyche, and is therefore, so to speak, a personality which we *also* are.'[2] Applied to psychology of religion, Jung's definition suggests that symbolism in the world's great faiths is a means by which the creative unconscious makes itself present to ego for the preservation and direction of the 'whole' human person. In fully developed form, this theory reflects Jung's interest in Eastern mysticism, where subordination of ego to self is a means of liberating the eternal principle in human nature from all that is transient and illusory. The 'integrated' personality, in short, is one wherein a reconciliation of conscious and unconscious elements is effected through self, and results in an experience of release and completeness. Jung's language is, furthermore, close to the recurring assertions of mystics that such experience is self-authenticating and self-evident: since the 'reality cannot be validated by any external criterion, any further attempt to describe and explain it is doomed to failure, for only those who have had this experience are in a position to understand and attest its reality'.[3]

As his letters to Fr Victor White[4] make clear, Jung did not consider himself a theologian, and would not say he had religious faith; only that he respected several religions, and, perhaps, that some kind of belief may be entailed in such an attitude. But for a theocentric tradition which affirms the mystery of Incarnation and God's creative freedom, the *summum bonum* is not just experience of an integrated self, but Beatific Vision in which human knowledge is infused by the self-communication of a transcendent God, and raised to heights of illumination inaccessible to our natural selves. Jung and the Christian mystics are not, however, altogether different: the mystics are merely explicit on a matter he does not consider a concern of natural science. Jung's attitude rather reflects the strong Kantian component in his early education. The non-phenomenal, Jung suggests, cannot be discussed scientifically; yet his theory remains carefully open to a noumenal reality which eludes the scientist's grasp.

If ego, then, is a centre of conscious life and a seat of moral responsibility, what should we make of advice that we must strive to open it to self – that it must be mortified, as the mystics say? 'I, Mine, Me, and the like', writes the author of the *Theologia Germanica*, are to be renounced, for 'nothing burneth in hell but self-will',[5] and Bérulle founded a tradition of mystical thought around his 'culte du non-moi'.

On this question, St Paul once more provides a key text: 'I live; yet not I, but Christ liveth in me' (Gal.: 2, 20). Ego is dangerous, that is, when it threatens to assert autonomy impeding expression of the personal Christ. John of Ruysbroeck talks of cutting to the very heart of such a tendency, because 'self-abasement', or 'the inward bowing down of the heart and of the conscience' is the foundation of all other virtues.[6]

Yet, in so far as civilisation promotes responsibility and science, it necessarily cultivates ego, and, clearly, ego's gifts cannot be rejected entirely. A panic-stricken leap into some crudely non-dualist philosophy would prove but meagre protection from problems to which the *cogito* gives rise. To annihilate ego would be to abandon lucidity and sense of purpose, the rule of ratio and the power of deliberate apprehension and analysis. Although sophisticated monist philosophies of the East may help to restore to the West some living sense of the spiritual pre-conscious as a corrective to a strong Western tendency to identify ego with self, the process should not require the West's intellectual achievements as forfeit.

'I, Mine, Me and the like', we conclude, ought not to be abhorrent to mystic vision because ego-consciousness is bad, but because of ego's *libido dominandi*: keen to grasp, ego excludes in order to differentiate, and proclaims its individuality, which, the theologians keep telling us, is not personality. The 'individual substance of a rational nature',[7] as Boethius' classic definition of 'person' has it, is aware both of differentiation between 'I' and its interlocutor, 'thou', and also of their communion. Boethius' definition occurs in a treatise on the Trinity, and it has been the special peculiarity of Christian thought to approach the unutterable mystery of Godhead itself through the category of persons. Within one divine nature, three persons, we are told, subsist in dynamic interchange of light, life and love, in which the Son, eternally dying to the Father, is resurrected in the Spirit.

Such high, if cryptic, value accorded to personality has encouraged Christians at best to consider all men equal in the sight of God, but it has also permitted Christians who do not happen to be theologically minded, to reduce their religion to a personality cult in a bad modern sense of the term,[8] reflecting the crudest kind of egotism. Clearly, one danger of theology defining its God in terms of persons is that it may invest ego-assertiveness with divine authority. Acquisitiveness, or any monstrous arrogance, can find it convenient to masquerade as righteous anger in the name of God who is too much like us. Theory, of course, has always made precise distinctions, as theories do. But anthropocentric suggestions in such doctrines as that of Atonement, whereby the Son's sacrifice is somehow made pleasing to the Father so that the devil's dues are paid, can scarcely be said to have discouraged a vicious practice, throughout history, whereby such satisfactions are exacted in turn on behalf of the Deity by his personal servants, the faithful, God's children, amidst fires and screams.

'Not I; but Christ liveth in me'; 'culte du non-moi'; 'nothing burneth in Hell but self will'; these, and countless statements like them throughout mystical literature, constitute a single voice of correction to all that would confuse the narrowness of ego in its vindictive, sentimental personalism and literal-mindedness, with the creative expansiveness of self. Mortification therefore is not just a matter of self-inflicted repressive penance: it is a

training in the harmony of human relationships, wherein we
relinquish desire to have power over others, or to control ourselves solely through ego. Jesus had done the will of the Father,
and his most readily ignored but central teaching is that, like him,
we are to be servants of servants. Christ's gift of the kingdom
within is offset, thus, by his insight into the perils of egotism that
attend such a gift, and the mystics, in this respect, are his most
ardent spokesmen.

Relinquishment of power over others should not, however, be
mistaken for passivity, the Quietist extreme which encourages
indifference to life-enhancing and active virtue. In not seeking
power, we are not powerless: rather, the power of another
moves in us. The 'naked intent stretching' described in the
anonymous *Epistle of Privy Counsel* is distinct from the 'false
vacancy'[9] which Ruysbroeck denounced; St John of the Cross,
with St Thomas, affirms that although we know God in Beatific
Vision without intermediary species or idea, the knowledge
remains active and intellectual.[10] 'Intent stretching' retains, in
some infinitely surprising degree, the synthesising activity
which seems to characterise the mind's most ordinary processes.

Indeed, the Jungian psychologist Erich Neumann argues that
homo mysticus is very much man in his everyday world, 'mystical'
in so far as he experiences the breakthrough of unconscious upon
ego, so that creative self is realised through a dialectical tension;
ego must not collapse before the invasion, but work to become a
vehicle of culture. Mystical experience consequently should
release to the world a divinely-strengthened personality able to
endure the tension between ego and self, in which ego is neither
congealed in marmorean autonomy nor disintegrated.

Mortification, then, is not mutilation, but pruning to produce
abundant fruit, and its true sense is given repeatedly in literature
where an artist's creative self finds expression, but not his ego or
mere individuality. Jacques Maritain is correct to suggest that
this is the way to read T.S. Eliot's essay in *The Sacred Wood*,
declaring the impersonality of art. Eliot claims the artist must cut
out of his work all traces of 'personality', but Eliot remains
innocent of the distinction between person and individual: when
the artist makes his personality 'extinct', as Eliot says, he should
be taken to mean that aspect of his personality which belongs to
the self-centred ego. Maritain goes on: 'that is to say of
individuality . . . . But at the same time the progress of an artist is

an ever more significant assertion of personality, that is to say of the creative subjectivity – revealed in the work together with things.'[11] Influenced by Maritain, but speaking from direct experience as both poet and painter, David Jones also insists on the importance of being dead to one's self, in the sense that ego is mortified in the act of creation. However egotistical the artist is in everyday life, in obedience to the skill at which he excels, that egotism is mortified: 'the workman must be dead to himself while engaged upon the work, otherwise we have that sort of "self-expression" which is as undesirable in the painter or the writer as in the carpenter, the half-back, or the cook.'[12] A sure sign of spurious art, in short, is that it calls attention to its own distinctiveness, to its author's individuality imposing itself rather than calling up from the reader a response of surprised recognition. In true art, creative self sets ablaze conscious ego to disclose something of the mysterious inner origins of nature's outward forms. Thus poet and mystic again beckon to each other, calling for a similar, attentive passivity that requires the ego mortified as a prior condition of illumination.

Literature of mysticism, therefore, will not only tell us about mortification, but also, at its best, will present us with an expression in which creative unconscious and personal vision assume the form of words. Boethius' *Consolation of Philosophy*, a work which has given to Western mystical tradition some key terms and insights for discussing the relationship of time to eternity, is relevant here because it is centrally concerned also with relationships of ego to self.

Boethius describes the predicament of a man unjustly imprisoned, anguished by loss of freedom, good name and material goods. In a dream, the man is instructed by Lady Philosophy that bondage to things of time – chattles, that is, of the whore Fortune – debilitates and corrupts the spirit. Happiness resides not in treacherous favours at the perimeter of Fortune's wheel, but at the centre, the still point of eternity. In the course of a series of conversations the imprisoned man is brought to re-evaluate his position, and to appreciate the eternal, because spiritual, nature of the human person, who must suffer the things of time, but whose essence transcends them.

To readers conversant with Jungian psychology, the appearance of a female dream figure in the first page of the *Consolation* would at once help to dramatise the exploration of self in a familiar manner. A Jungian would recognise Lady Philosophy as *anima* in the benevolent sense, and Lady Fortune, her counterpart, as negative *anima*. The prisoner is required to give allegiance to one or the other, and throughout the *Consolation* the theme of return from a place of exile or imprisonment to one's true home is carefully developed. A rich but severe series of contrasts between images, for instance, suggests alternative directions of the prisoner's allegiance either towards egotistical self-indulgence, or towards the spiritual resources which enable him to be more than a victim of his circumstances. So, placed against Fortune's wheel, perpetually deceptive, is the image of an orb of light, true source of knowledge and illumination, and the dialogue form itself enacts the conflict through which a way towards the centre is discovered, as does the alternation of verse and prose. Throughout, allusions to sickness and health suggest the ordeal of body, soul and spirit yearning towards wholeness, which is holiness, health of the person, the book's theme.

We are, furthermore, led through an imagined density of 'external' circumstances, working our way as we read, as it were, from circumference to centre. Book I is heavily biographical, most full of complaint and concerned with outward trappings of the prisoner's life and circumstances. Book II remains on the circumference, but, by discussing the fickleness of fortune, leads us towards the interior life, suggesting that happiness is within. In Book III the prisoner feels stronger, and begins actively to contribute to Lady Philosophy's advice. In Book IV he is able to discuss evil and injustice, concluding that the moral sickness of evil men is more terrible than the suffering of their victims. In Book V, the debate opens out with leisurely ease upon the question of eternity, ending with a discussion of the Judge whose vision encompasses all times.

As the argument progresses, understanding deepens in proportion to mortification of the merely 'external' man and the relinquishment of his ego-assertiveness. So also, Boethius' use of poetry, serving to introduce or conclude an argument, is suggestively varied. Book I begins and ends with verse; Books II, III and IV begin with prose and end with verse. Book V neither begins nor ends with verse. It is as if the prisoner interiorises the power of poetry as he grows more active in understanding what philosophy has to tell him. Poetry's images attest for him the spirituality of knowledge, but yield, as it were, before intel-

lectual vision. We have, in so far as words can suggest such a
thing, thus worked to the centre, in Book v, where discussion of
eternity corresponds to a still point at the wheel's axis, centre of
the orb, the homeland, the self, centre of light, and of freedom
achieved through a progressive mortification of ego.

My second example of a mystical author concerned to show
through imagination the self's creative intuition is William Law
(1686–1761), who did not live in an age of faith, but in an age free
to disbelieve, so that his writing shows us with particular clarity
the challenge posed for ego by faith.

Law, says Charles Williams, wrote a small number of books
which 'form perhaps one of the best statements of the pure
Christian religion that have ever been issued.[13] The best-known
is perhaps *A Serious Call to a Devout and Holy Life*, which is concerned with practical Christianity, claiming that peace and
happiness on earth depend on devotion to God informing our
every action. Law does not just denounce worldliness, but sets it
out before us 'by looking at that which is contrary';[14] that is, by
displaying, with wit and precision, a series of satirical portraits of
those who have dedicated themselves to the varieties of an
illusory 'gewgaw happiness'.[15] Dr Johnson recalls picking up the
Serious Call 'expecting to find it a dull book (as such books
generally are), and perhaps to laugh at it. But,' he concludes, 'I
found Law's quite an overmatch for me.'[16]

From Dr Johnson to Aldous Huxley, Law has had admirers,
and the literary qualities of the *Serious Call* have a good deal to do
with his success. The prose is forceful, clear, elegant and witty. It
has the Enlightenment virtues of forthrightness, reasonableness
and commonsense. It has, stylistically, the firmness of the moral
life it prescribes, communicating a quality of voice and mind in
tune with its own good reasons.

But although the *Serious Call* made Law famous, it is not the
fullest expression of his vision, and the change between what
might be described as 'early' and 'late' phases of his career can be
located in a single event, which occurred when Law was about 50
years of age. On casually picking up a book by the High German
mystic Jacob Boehme (1515–1624), Law fell 'into a *perfect
sweat*',[17] and although the principles of his earlier teaching were
not changed by a subsequent absorbtion of Boehme's thought,
they were filled out and deepened. C. S. Lewis has this to say of
Law's *Appeal to All Who Doubt the Truths of the Gospel*:

I . . . like it as well as any religious work I have ever read. The *prose* of the *Serious Call* has here been all melted away and the book is saturated with delight and the sense of wonder; one of those rare works which make you say of Christianity, 'Here is the very thing you like in poetry and the romances, but this time it's true'.[18]

Law's late, post-Boehme prose is, in short, poetic.

At this point, some knowledge of Boehme would help, but, except in a small way, such a subject is beyond the scope of this chapter.[19] Briefly, however, although Boehme's formal education was slight, he seems to have come into contact with the main traditions of Western mysticism from the Fathers to Thomas à Kempis, and there is reason to believe he was learned in Renaissance Platonism and alchemy, and had read widely in contemporary scientific thought. That his personal vision of the 'ground and the unground', the 'birth of the holy Trinity', and the fall of angels and men is highly original will be immediately clear to his most casual reader. We learn of the Abyss of Godhead, the Triune Principle which becomes manifest through Seven Properties, three of which are dark and three light, with the mediating fourth, the 'lightning flash' as agent which turns dark towards light. The Seven Properties act harmoniously in eternal nature, and the arrangement in sets of opposed pairs enables Boehme to get across his key idea that manifestation involves duality: as Boehme's most famous English disciple, William Blake, was later to put it, 'Without Contraries is no progression'.[20]

We learn also of a fall of angels and men in context of the Trinity which consists of the Father's fire softened by the Son's light, with Spirit mediating between them. The angelic world, we are told, fell when Lucifer's jealousy of the Son caused the fire-principle to burn up in himself as wrath, precipitating a catastrophic chain-reaction through creation. We learn of a second creation, and of Adam's fall from the androgynous state of his paradisal body, into the divisions and separations to which flesh is heir, and how the material world subsequently was crystallised out by God into its present form, to mark a limit to the fall. Christ, the cosmic redeemer whose seed is in each of us, was afterwards born as a man to conquer the fiery self-will, and passed through the states of fallen human nature, at last reassuming, after death, the paradisal body, an act by which all men are summoned, and directed.

Law slaked himself on Boehme, partly because he found there a complete system, or cosmic myth rooted in tradition and yet informed by personal vision which seemed to him reassuringly coherent, and deeply satisfying. The early Law, for all his criticism of Enlightenment complacency, had shared the high evaluation his contemporaries placed on commonsense, clear argument, and reason. His was the age of Newton, whom he admired, and of Rationalism, which he studied. And yet, the incapacity of science and reason to penetrate the mystery of human consciousness was never absent from his mind: the 'Wrangle of a rational Debate' is ever distinct from 'a *living Sensibility* of the Power, Life, and Religion of Love'.[21] The *Serious Call* keeps reminding us of this difference, and Law well understood that he must find a way to retain the certainties of Newtonian science and of clear argument (the function of ego), while proclaiming the energy of creative spirit (the function of self).

Initially, to this end, Law studied Malebranche, who, among the Cartesian rationalists, became his favourite. Malebranche, we recall from the previous chapter, accepted Descartes' rationalist spirit, but feared lest the full-blown Cartesian theory would encourage man to ignore God and assume Luciferan autonomy. In the end, however, Law acknowledged also the deficiencies of Malebranche, and in the *Spirit of Love* criticised 'the Schools of *Descartes, Malebranche* or *Locke*' for not adequately knowing the 'Ground' (p. 15) of spirit or body which they yoked together in too arbitrary a manner. Boehme, in short, had by now come to do for Law what Malebranche had done less well: he provided a myth, rooted in traditional knowledge, and yet, in Law's hands, able to accommodate Newton's insights. That Law was especially eager to take Boehme's thought in this direction is evident from the curious (historically unproven) insistence that Newton had gained the basis for his own great discoveries from reading Boehme: in explaining the 'Laws of *Matter* and *Motion*,' Law confides, 'the illustrious Sir *Isaac* plowed with *Behmen's* Heifer' (p. 19).

Malebranche served Law less well than Boehme, we can conjecture, because the 'occasionalist' theory was itself too rationalist: the model remains artificial and mechanical, and merely synchronises us with our world. Boehme, however, provided a system which acted as a symbol of faith itself, and which enabled the poet to place himself in a personally satisfying way within the world's mystery, thereby releasing ego of its burden of self-consciousness. Such a myth alone does not make a poet, nor can a poet simply invent such a myth, because then he could not give himself up to it. But having received it, as a wholly satisfying symbol of faith and of mortified ego, the creative energy of self is set free. In some such manner, Boehme's system allowed Law's imagination to move with new expansiveness and delight, between the mystery of unmanifest abyssal Deity, and the Newtonian world of concrete reality. For Law, Boehme spoke as truly as Newton and about the same things, as we are urged to recognise. Indeed, a constant theme of *The Spirit of Love*, is that a Boehemist Christianity accounts for the laws of nature: 'You are to know, *Eusebius*, that the Christian Religion is no *arbitrary System* of Divine Worship, but is the one true, real, and only Religion of Nature; that is, it is wholly founded in the Nature of Things, has nothing in it supernatural, or contrary to the Powers and Demands of Nature; but all that it does, is only in, and by, and according to the Workings and Possibilities of Nature' (p. 90). And although Law talks often of 'imagination' in a negative sense (using it indiscriminately with the word 'Fiction' to indicate a mere disembodied notion), *The Spirit of Love* is itself imaginative. As Law puts it, things 'must be in restless Strife and Disquiet' (p. 8) until that *'glassy sea* of Unity' (p. 9) is achieved, and the arguments of Theophilus, Law's spokesman, are full of imaginative strokes intended to bring his interlocutors to one mind with himself.

It is difficult to give, in brief compass, a sense of Law's range and humane insight, but there is a certain grand dimension, for instance, to his late work, discussing the cosmic Christ, the birth of darkness and light, the properties of fire as the root of wrath and divine energy. And when one turns to his doctrine of Atonement, it is satisfying to feel how sound are Law's applications of such cosmic mythology to the old juridical teaching which he deplores. Christ, we learn, is the seed of God in man, and began to restore nature from the first reassuring words spoken to Adam: Christ, in short, is all the energy that would set nature right. Atonement therefore 'declares a God, that is all Love', and is

Nothing else in itself, but the highest, most natural, and efficacious Means, through all the Possibility of Things, that the infinite Love and Wisdom of God could use, to put an End to Sin, and Death, and Hell, and restore to Man his first Divine State or Life. I say, the most natural, efficacious Means through *all the Possibilities of* Nature; for there is nothing that is *supernatural*, however mysterious, in the whole System of our Redemption; every Part of it has its Ground in the Workings and Powers of Nature, and all our Redemption is only Nature set right, or made to be that which it ought to be. (p. 83)

Through such a process, Law holds that Jesus realised Christ by enduring the worst that fallen Nature's selfish, fiery wrath could do to him as a Son of Man who maintained, despite his pains, the original spirit of Adam. This is suffering on our *account*, not *in our place*, and humanity therefore continues to stand, with Jesus, in the midst of nature's contraries, out of which, in Blakean fashion, it can make a heaven or hell, so that Law's insistence on a perpetual inner resistance to wrath and selfishness is characteristically irradiated by an intense vision of nature as the mirror of man's desires:

I said the *Serpents* of Covetousness, Envy, Pride, and Wrath, because they are alone the *real, dreadful, original* Serpents; and all earthly Serpents are but transitory, partial, and weak Out-Births of them. All evil earthly Beasts, are but short-lived Images, or creaturely Eruptions of that hellish Disorder, that is broken out from the fallen spiritual World; and by their manifold Variety, they show us that *Multiplicity* of Evil, that lies in the Womb of that Abyss of dark Rage, which (*N.B.*) has *no Maker*, but the three first Properties of Nature, fallen from God, and working in their own Darkness.

So that all evil, mischievous, ravenous, venomous Beasts, though they have no Life, but what begins in and from this material World, and totally ends at the Death of their Bodies, yet have they no Malignity in their earthly temporary Nature, but from those *same wrathful* Properties of fallen Nature, which *live* and *work* in our eternal fallen Souls. And therefore, though they are as different from us, as Time from Eternity, yet wherever we see them we see so many infallible Proofs of the *Fall* of Nature, and the *Reality* of Hell. For was there no Hell broken out in spiritual Nature, not only no evil Beast, but no bestial Life, could ever have come into Existence. (pp. 120–1)

An endemic fault of the kind of idealism that would suggest serpents are not real is to underestimate the real horror they can inspire, in face of which we resort to anything but the consolations of idealism. But in this passage, as throughout his writings, Law's indignation at the 'malignity' of the beasts remains vehement and sufficiently close to the surface, so that the underlying wrathful powers are glimpsed as an energy sustaining the manifest terror from which we are *not* asked entirely to shift attention. 'What a really wonderful writer', says Aldous Huxley, 'it is sadly typical of our education that we are all made to read the second-rate amiabilities of Addison and Steele – but that one of the great masters of devotion and of philosophical theology is passed over almost in silence.'[22]

The passing of an 'age of faith' before an age of science, we might say, entails the fact that myths expressing faith are now to be freely chosen as well as inherited. Not all myths, of course, are equally germane to all people, and some readers of Boehme, for instance, find only rubbish. But Law found a means to enrich his vision with charity and tolerance, fruits of the truly mortified ego, and, also, to reconcile the gifts of Newton with the spiritual traditions of the Christian past. 'Doctrines of Religion I have none, but what the Scriptures and *first-rate* Saints of the Church are Vouchers for',[23] Law proclaims, including among his saints the 'deep mystic writers of the Romish Church'.[24] The best teachers of essential Christianity, he came to see, were other mystics like himself. The result is a unique vision, embodying the modern truth that in a secular age vital relationship to tradition needs to be self-conscious, a matter of free imitation creatively directing the imagination as a means of opening ego to self. In such circumstances, traditional faith is available to an especially wide variety of sensibilities, and traditional teachings thus formulated to encounter the challenge of secularism can often be discovered to possess an unexpected subtlety and depth. This is the case, as we see, with Law's interpretation of Atonement, in which he rejects as a wretched 'fiction' all teachings based on judicial satisfaction or appeasement of the Father's wrath.

Boethius and Law both tell us of mortification, and their

poetry conveys the experience of an emergent, creative self following upon renunciation of egotism. Mortification, in this sense, is more than crude asceticism, even though asceticism is implied in it. On the natural level it is like the behaviour of a man with a heart problem, who submits to a programme of physical exercise. Should he strain too much he will do himself the very injury he wishes to avoid. So may the ego call attention to itself by the very extremity of acts undertaken to tame it, and one can grow hard in ascetic virtue. The runner suffers, rather, to avoid damaging his weak heart, and to keep its arteries open; likewise the fulfilment of natural asceticism is to keep open in body and mind to the possibility of revelation. We are advised, simply, to renounce that which impedes the disposition of man to truth, or prevents the development of an integrated humanity. 'He was no friend of immoderate fasting', writes the biographer and disciple of St Francois de Sales, 'and gives this reason against the practice. "When the body is over-fed, the mind cannot support its weight; but when the body is weak and wasted, it cannot support the mind."'[25]

No doubt, asceticism does remind us of mortality, and has often been practised and recommended by spiritual writers as a kind of training for death, rather than an encouragement to life-enhancing engagement of the world. In Christian tradition, the passion of Jesus is thus the foremost example of mortification, and ascetic theology, not surprisingly, looks to the passion for guidance. Christ's abandonment, we are told, was to the uttermost, and, as that life is to be the pattern of human experience, so when we die we must also endure the ego's powerlessness. As St John of the Cross tells us, in the mystical death of the Dark Night, one feels that God has abandoned the soul.[26] But only ego's pride and weakness, this teaching also implies, seek to defeat death by somehow obliterating ego. The Pauline sense of dying into Christ is quite different, and involves precisely a relinquishment of the desire to effect one's own salvation, which the techniques of ego-obliteration imply. In Western tradition, the way of the cross and the mystic way are therefore not only analogous: they meet in the existential act of dying. A person's death is real because he is conscious of it, though powerless, 'being-unto-death', in Heidegger's phrase.

There are, consequently, three attitudes. The first refuses the possibility of meaning, and faces death in despair. The second attempts to deny death victory by an act of will turned inward to enforce ego's dissolution. The third undertakes . death with conscious acceptance, with the soul's cry of faith at Annunciation, 'Be it done unto me according to thy word', sustained to the end. And because Christianity chooses the third attitude, Christian mysticism characteristically takes the cross as a central subject of meditation, as Christ also took it, in full consciousness, as the way of mortification. The narrow grasping of ego clearly is not served by such an act, and ego pre-eminently may be said to be crucified. But not annihilated: rather, because conscious, it is brought up against the supreme possibility that the self-communication of some Other, whom death puts most terribly in question, is the fulfilment of its hope and faith.

Asceticism, therefore, is a free participation in the fate of human life, which is death. Its aim is not to defeat death in the sense of foiling it by magical practice aimed at collapsing or disintegrating the ego. Consciousness is rather strengthened through Christ, by release from its own narrowness and rigidity, and the balance, as always, is the perilous synthesis of a poem's disciplined spontaneity: its particular but never egocentric voice, its uniqueness, its world–transforming energy.

In conclusion, mystical tradition of the Latin West does not encourage us to identify self with God, but affirms that we are God-like. It describes God in terms of Persons and Nature, but insists that divine transcendence calls upon man's faith, outside of which it is futile to seek life's meaning. It acknowledges itself within history, but not of it. It calls for mortification of the ego, but not obliteration of consciousness. It enjoins an ascesis whereby the way of solitude prepares for personal acceptance, attentively passive, distinct from the way of individuality, desirous of power. It suggests that the dynamic inter-relationship of self and ego calls for the tact of a poet whose syntax is life, and whose goal is the completely real.

TEXTS WITHOUT COMMENT

4 SELF AND EGO

PRIDE AND HUMILITY

1. Men might see this very clearly, if they would but reflect on
    that feeling of dislike and aversion produced in them by
    those, who do not commend their spirit, or attribute no
    value to their experiences, and on that feeling of distress,
    which they have when they are told that others also have the
    like or greater gifts. All this is the fruit of secret self-esteem
    and pride, and they cannot be made to understand that they
    are steeped in it up to their very eyes. They think that a
    certain recognition of their own wretchedness is sufficient,
    while at the same time they are filled with secret self-esteem
    and personal satisfaction, taking more delight in their own
    spirit and gifts than in those of another. They are like the
    Pharisee who thanked God that he was 'not as the rest of
    men,' and that he practised such and such virtues: he was
    satisfied with himself, and presumed upon his state.

    John of the Cross (1542–91),
    Ascent of Mount Carmel, III, 8

2. Art not Thou the Creator of the world, the beauty of
    Heaven, the Paradise of Angels, the redemption of man-
    kind, the splendour of Thy Father's glory, the fountain of
    Divine Wisdom in its depths? How canst Thou will to wash
    my feet, Thou Lord of so great majesty and glory, how
    canst Thou desire to take upon Thee a service so low?

    Peter of Alcantara (1499–1562),
    A Golden Treatise of Mental Prayer, I, 4

3. Be not willing to be as it were thine own and in thine own
    control; but profess thyself to be the bondman of that most
    clement and most profitable Lord. For so will He not desist
    from lifting thee to Himself, and will suffer nothing to occur
    to thee, except what shall profit thee, even though thou
    know it not.

    Augustine of Hippo (354–430),
    Soliloquies, XV, 30

4. Be assured, he who helpeth a man to his own will, helpeth

him to the worst that he can. For the more a man followeth
after his own self-will, and self-will groweth in him, the
farther off is he from God, the true Good, for nothing
burneth in hell but self-will. Therefore it hath been said, 'Put
off thine own will, and there will be no hell'. Now God is
very willing to help a man and bring him to that which is
best in itself, and is of all things the best for man. But to this
end, all self-will must depart, as we have said.

Theologia Germanica (c. 1350), Ch. xxxiv

5. It hath been said, that there is of nothing so much in hell as of
self-will. The which is true, for there is nothing else there
than self-will, and if there were no self-will there would be
no Devil and no hell.

Theologia Germanica (c. 1350), Ch. xlix

6. For these causes therfore I say not that wee must behold the
will of God in our worke or intention, but I say wee must
behold the worke or intention as the verie will of God,
which is God himself, whoe by his presence doth anihillate
in this respect both the worke, and intention or will of man;
not that indeed they are nothing (having always their
essence) but that they are so little that in comparison and the
presence of God they are nothing; and though they be some
thing, yet must they not heer be seene as such, but as
nothing; because though in it self the worke be some thing,
yet considered in the will of God, it is nothing, but even the
same will of God into which it is transformed, and so of
death and darknes is made life and brightnes, and that which
in it self was corporall, in the will of God is made spirituall.

Benet of Canfield (1520–1611),
Rule of Perfection, i, 14

7. For he is an arrogant spirit and hates littleness, because it
serves towards humility – he who has always loved pride,
haughtiness, and arrogance, and who, because he would not
stay in his littleness, lost his greatness. Labour in humility,
in abjection; let people talk and act as they will.

François de Sales (1567–1622),
Letters to Persons in Religion, iii, 43

8. The humilities which are least seen are the finest.

François de Sales (1567–1622),
Letters to Persons in Religion, iv, 34

9. Observe, my brethren, how humility justifies us. Humility,

I say, not humiliation. How many there are who suffer humiliation without being humble!

Bernard of Clairvaux (1091–1153),
Sermons on the Canticles, XXXIV

10. Wherefore, Brethren, if we desire to reach the eminence of Humility, and arrive soon at the very top of that heavenly ascent, to which we can only climb by the lowliness of this present life; we must ascend by good works, and erect the mystical Ladder of Jacob, where Angels ascending and descending were represented to him. Doubtless nothing else is meant by that ascent and descent, but that we go downward when we exalt our selves, and rise when we are humbled. The Ladder represents our life in this world which our Lord erects to Heaven when the heart is humbled. And the sides of it bear resemblance with our soul and body between which God has placed several degrees of humility and observance, whereby we are to ascend in order to pursue his divine call.

Benedict (c. 480–c. 547)
Rule, 7

11. And so when these and such like faults which are also visible to the eyes of men, are entirely removed and cut off, and when such a purification and cleansing, as we spoke of, has first taken place, which is brought about by pure simplicity and innocence, then first there must be laid the secure foundations of a deep humility, which may be able to support a tower that shall reach the sky.

John Cassian (c. 360–435),
Conferences, IX, 3

12. Be then busy to get meekness [i.e. humility], and hold it; for it is the first and the last of all virtues. It is the first, for it is the ground of all, as Saint Austin saith: 'If thou think to build an high house of virtues, ordain thee first a deep ground of meekness'. Also it is the last, for it is the keeping and saving of all other virtues, as Saint Gregory saith: 'He that gathereth virtues without meekness, he is like to him which maketh and beareth powder of spicery in the wind'. Do thou never so many good deeds – fast thou, wake thou, or any other good works do thou – if thou have no meekness it is naught that thou dost.

Walter Hilton (–1396),
Scale of Perfection, I, 18

13. Humility may be defined, to be a vertue by which wee acknowledging the Infinite greatnes and Majesty of God, his incomprehensible Perfections, and the absolute Power that he hath over us and all creatures (which are as nothing before him) doe wholly subject our selves, both soules and bodies, with all their powers and faculties, and all things that pertaine to either, to his holy will in all things, and for his sake to all creatures according to his will.

Augustine Baker (1575–1641),
Sancta Sophia, Treatise II, 424

MORTIFICATION

14. The first Difference is, that they who mortifie themselves with their own proper industry, are presumptuous, & ambitious, knowing their own proper vertue in their mortification; and they who are mortified by the holy spirit, are humble, and modest, not knowing any proper virtue of their own in their mortifications: for the holy spirit works in them that which a very great Feaver doth in a man.

Juan de Valdes (1490–1541),
Considerations, LVIII

15. So long as thou art capable of anything against the will of God and against his law thou hast no love of God though thou cozen the world that thou hast it. One who is in God's will and in God's love is fain to do the things God likes and leave undone the things God hates, and he can no more leave undone a thing that God wants done than he can do a thing that God abhors; just like a man whose legs are tied together, he cannot stray and neither can he err who is in the will of God. Someone once said, 'God may command me to do evil and shun virtue, but I am incapable of sin'. No one loves virtue without being virtue. He who abandons himself and everything, who seeks not his own in any wise but does all he does for love and without why, that man being dead to all the world is alive in God and God in him.

Meister Eckhart (1260–1327),
Sermons and Collations, LXXIV,
'The Promise of the Father'

16. Our holy and most ascetic master stated that the monk

should always live as if he were to die on the morrow but at the same time that he should treat his body as if he were to live on with it for many years to come. For, he said, by the first attitude he will be able to cut off every thought that comes from *acedia* and thus become more fervent in his monastic practices, by the second device he will preserve his body in good health and maintain its continence intact.

Evagrius Ponticus (345–99),
Praktikos, 29

17. For on this account one is anxious to secure and provide for one's self the implements for any branch of work, not simply to possess them to no purpose, nor as if one made the profit and advantage, which is looked for from them, to consist in the bare fact of possession but that by using them, one may effectually secure practical knowledge and the end of that particular art of which they are auxiliaries. Therefore, fastings, vigils, meditation on the Scriptures, self-denial, and the abnegation of all possessions are not perfection, but aids to perfection: because the end of that science does not lie in these, but by means of these we arrive at the end. He then will practise these.

John Cassian (c. 360–435),
Conferences, I, 7

18. When maidens are always clothed according to the will of their Bridegroom, they need nothing but the Bridal-gown; that is to say they are rich in pain, illness, days of sadness, temptation and the many kinds of suffering we find in sinful Christianity. These are the wedding-garments of the loving soul.

Mechthild of Magdeburg (1212–99),
Revelations, Part 7, 65

19. The darkness, of which the soul here speaks, relates, as I have said, to the desires, and to the interior sensitive and spiritual powers, which are all to be deprived of their natural light in this night; so that, being purified herein, they may be supernaturally enlightened. The sensitive and spiritual desires are lulled to sleep and mortified, unable to relish anything either human or Divine: the affections are thwarted and brought low, incapable of excitement, and having nothing to rest upon; the imagination is fettered, and unable to make any profitable reflections, the memory is

gone, the intellect is obscured, and the will, too, is dry and afflicted, and all the faculties are empty, and, moreover, a dense and heavy cloud overshadows the wearied soul, and alienates it, as it were, from God. This is the obscurity in which the soul says that it travels securely.

John of the Cross (1542–91),
Obscure Night of the Soul, II, 16

20. This poor soul, after having lost its all, must at last lose its own life by an utter self-despair, or rather it must die worn out by a terrible fatigue. Prayer in this degree is extremely painful, because the soul being no longer able to make use of its own powers, of which it seems to be entirely deprived, and God having taken from it a certain sweet and profound calm which supported it, is left like those poor children whom we see running here and there in search of bread, yet finding no one to supply their need, so that the power of prayer seems to be as entirely lost as if we had never possessed it; but with this difference, that we feel the pain occasioned by the loss, because we have proved its value by its possession, while others are not sensible of the loss, because they have never known its enjoyment. The soul, then, can find no support in the creature; and if it feels itself carried away by the things of earth, it is only by impetuosity, and it can find nothing to satisfy it. Not that it does not seek to abandon itself to the things in which it formerly delighted; but alas! it finds in them nothing but bitterness, so that it is glad to leave them again, taking nothing back but sadness at its own unfaithfulness.

Madame Guyon (1648–1717),
Spiritual Torrents, VII, 4

21. I fasted much, and walked abroad in solitary places many days, and often took my Bible, and went and sat in hollow trees and lonesome places till night came on; and frequently, in the night, walked mournfully about by myself: for I was a man of sorrows in the times of the first workings of the Lord in me.

George Fox (1642–90),
Journal, entry for 1647

22. Being Swallowed up therfore in the Miserable Gulph of idle talk and worthless vanities, thenceforth I lived among Shadows, like a Prodigal Son feeding upon Husks with

Swine. A Comfortless Wilderness full of Thorns and Troubles the World was, or wors: a Waste Place covered with Idleness and Play, and Shops and Markets and Taverns. As for Churches they were things I did not understand. And Scholes were a Burden: so that there was nothing in the World worth the having, or Enjoying, but my Game and Sport, which also was a Dream and being passed wholy forgotten. So that I had utterly forgotten all Goodness Bounty Comfort and Glory: which things are the very Brightness of the Glory of GOD: for lack of which therfore He was unknown.

Thomas Traherne (1637–74),
Centuries, III, 14

RELINQUISHMENT

23. If thou consider the time, before thou wast, thou shalt see, that in all that eternitie, thou wast a meere nothing, and that thou didst not worke, or couldest woorke any thing to deserve thy being. In this time after sithence that by the only goodnesse of God thou hast thy being, leaving to god that which is his: (that is, the continuall governements, with the which he ruleth and preserveth thee) with that which thou hast of thy selfe, what other thing art thou, but in like maner a nothing? It is therefore evident, that in this thy first naturall being, standing with thine owne, thou hast not in any respect reason to esteeme thy selfe, or to desire to bee esteemed of others.

Lorenzo Scupoli (1530–1610),
The Spiritual Conflict, 19

24. Yes – I am still a pacifist though I agree with you about the increasing difficulty of it. But I feel more and more sure that Christianity and war are incompatible, and that *nothing* worth having can be achieved by 'casting out Satan by Satan'. All the same, I don't think pacifists at the moment should be controversial, or go in for propaganda. The nation as a whole obviously feels it right to fight this war out, and must I think do it. I think Hitler is a real 'scourge of God', the permitted judgment on our civilisation; and there are only two ways of meeting him – war, or the Cross. And

only a very small number are ready for the Cross, in the full sense of loving and unresisting abandonment to the worst that may come. So those who see that this alone is *full* Christianity should be careful not to increase the disharmony of life by trying to force this difficult truth on minds that are closed against it, and will only be exasperated by it. At present I think one can do little but try to live in charity, and do what one can for the suffering and bewildered. We are caught up in events far too great for us to grasp, and which have their origin in the 'demonic powers' of the spiritual world. Let us hope that the end of all the horror and destruction may be a purification of life!

Evelyn Underhill (1875–1941),
Letters, to Mildred Bosanquet, 12 May 1941

25. No one who loves true prayer and yet gives way to anger or resentment can be absolved from the imputation of madness. For he resembles a man who wishes to see clearly and for this purpose he scratches his eyes.

Evagrius Ponticus (345–99),
Chapters on Prayer, 64

26. This work of compassion and of common neighbourly love overcomes and casts out the third mortal sin, that is hatred or Envy. For compassion is a wound in the heart, whence flows a common love to all mankind and which cannot be healed so long as any suffering lives in man; for God has ordained grief and sorrow of heart before all the virtues.

John of Ruysbroeck (1293–1381),
*The Adornment of the Spiritual
Marriage*, Ch. xviii

27. Son, be not curious: nor trouble thyself with idle anxieties. What is this or that to thee: follow thou Me. For what is it to thee whether that man be such or such; or this man do or speak this or that? Thou needest not answer for others: but shalt give account for thyself. Why then dost thou entangle thyself?

Thomas à Kempis (1380–1471), *Of the
Imitation of Christ*, Bk. iii, Ch. 24

28. Think no further of thyself than I bid thee do of thy God, so that thou be one with him in spirit as thus, without any separating and scattering of mind. For he is thy being, and in him thou art what thou art, not only by cause and by being,

but also he is in thee both thy cause and thy being. And therefore think of God in thy work as thou dost on thyself, and on thyself as thou dost on God: that he is as he is and thou art as thou art; so that thy thought be not scattered nor separated, but oned in him that is all; evermore saving this difference betwixt thee and him, that he is thy being and thou not his.

Epistle of Privy Counsel (late 14th C.), Ch. 1

29. Behold, these men have gone astray into the vacant and blind simplicity of their own being, and they seek for blessedness in bare nature; for they are so simply and so idly united with the bare essence of their souls, and with that wherein God always is, that they have neither zeal, nor cleaving to God, neither from without, nor from within. For in the highest part into which they have entered, they feel nothing but the simplicity of their own proper being, depending upon the Being of God. And the onefold simplicity which they there possess, they take to be God, because they find a natural rest therein. And so they think themselves to be God in their simple ground.

John of Ruysbroeck (1293–1381),
The Book of Supreme Truth, Ch. iv

30. For because Religion is justly placed in the heart, some have pursued that notion so far, as to renounce vocal prayer, and other outward acts of worship, and have resolved all religion into a quietism, or mystic intercourse with God in silence. Now these are two extremes equally prejudicial to true Religion; and ought not to be objected either against internal, or external worship. As you ought not to say, that I encourage that quietism by placing religion in the heart: so neither ought you to say, that I encourage superstition, by showing the benefit of outward acts of worship. For since we are neither all soul, nor all body; seeing none of our actions are either separately of the soul, or separately of the body; seeing we have no habits but such as are produced by the actions both of our souls and bodies; it is certain, that if we would arrive at habits of devotion, or delight in God, we must not only meditate and exercise our souls, but we must practise and exercise our bodies to all such outward actions, as are conformable to these inward tempers.

William Law (1686–1761),
A Serious Call, Ch. xv

CHAPTER FIVE
The Cross

The cross, then, is central to Christian mysticism. Thomas à Kempis assures us:

> You cannot escape it, whithersoever you run. For wheresoever you go you carry yourself with you, and shall always find yourself. Turn upwards or turn downwards, turn inwards or turn outwards: everywhere, you shall find the cross.[1]

We are to graft ourselves to Christ crucified because the way to glory is through humility, says Meister Eckhart. 'Let Christ crucified be sufficient for thee', writes St John of the Cross, whose terse advice is affirmed repeatedly by writers in the spiritual tradition down to our own time: Paul Tillich claims that profession of Christ which does not submit to Jesus crucified is idolatry, for the cross is Christianity's unique symbol; Jurgen Moltmann says it is the key to Christian Theology.[2]

But the cross depicts horror, and it is perplexing to understand how meditation on a torture can edify. Trinitarian theology admittedly maintains that Father and Son are equally one God, but popular attention has always been drawn to the plainer fact that the Son, not the Father, is crucified. The powerful phantasm of a son's tormented humanity forsaken, at last, by His Father in heaven confirms this distinction of persons more strongly than mandarin theology proves their identity. Certainly, Christians have often found it difficult to put back together, as mystery, what imagination has put apart, and rack and gallows have often re-enacted the cross in the name of omnipotence, attempting to enforce conformity to a divine will conceived in the image of vindictive personalism.

To what extent, in Christian history, such anthropomorphic

simplification has catered merely to human vanity and cruelty is impossible to say, but it is evidently great. The kind of thinking, for instance, that forbade Jews to live as equals among Christians because the cross was their stumbling block, could readily enough yield the conclusion that Jews may be forbidden to live at all. But not only Jews: Muslims, Cathars, Arians, Gnostics, Baptists, Catholics, Protestants, witches, homosexuals, saints – all *anathema* and bearers of heresy through history have fallen beneath swords of righteousness wielded in the name of the cross, the sign of a son's immolated flesh offered to his satisfied father.[3]

Speaking for the best insight of a spiritual tradition opposed to such enormities William Law has offered a diagnosis and a warning:

> say, with the current of scholastic Divines, That Sin must be doomed to eternal Pain and Death, unless a supposed Wrath, in the Mind of the Deity, be first atoned and satisfied; and that Christ's Death was that valuable Gift, or Offering made to God, by which alone he could be moved to lay aside, or extinguish his own Wrath towards fallen Man; say this, and then you open a wide Door for Licentiousness and Infidelity in some, and superstitious Fears in others.
>
> For if the Evil, the Misery, and sad Effects of Sin, are placed in a Wrath in the Divine Mind, what can this beget in the Minds of the pious, but superstitious Fears about a supposed Wrath in God which they can never know when it is, or is not atoned? Every Kind of Superstition has its Birth from this Belief, and cannot well be otherwise.[4]

Decent and moral Christian lives have of course been lived despite the unlovely historical facts, but the mystics especially provide grounds for an understanding that may suffice, not to redeem wrong done in the name of the cross, but to show what the cross means, and how we are to accept it.

First, we are to understand that signs regarded for their own sake lead to idolatry. In the moment of union, Bonaventure tells us, the cross passes away, as does all manner of thinking in and through signs, for we know the One God immediately and ineffably.[5] Although St Teresa advises, 'Fix your eyes on the Crucified and nothing else will be of much importance to you', she assures us that in the Prayer of Union, the Persons of the Trinity are experienced in a manner beyond imagination as 'one Substance and one Power and one Knowledge and one God alone'.[6] For these writers the Cross represents the incomplete nature of whatever in space and time impedes our intuition of Deity. As Paul Tillich says, the Cross is Christianity's foremost sign because, in representing the insufficiency of signs, it calls most directly upon faith in the unseen reality. All our makings and doings consequently take on value as acts of giving-over, of self-dedication to the end beyond the end of Art and Culture and Civilisation, the Absolute beyond time.

Throughout the Middle Ages in books of hours and *specula*, illuminated manuscripts, sculpture, tapestries, and poetry, the rood tree in some such sense remains the sign of man's journey through fallen history. It branches through the divisions of time, as *arbor vitae* and axis of the world; it is the ship of faith manned by Christ: 'portum petitis? / Non transibitis/Sine crucis navi'.[7] Yet the cross in Christian tradition is not just a sign; it is also a historical event. As such, Christians have commemorated it and brooded on it, and often have refused to let it take its place in the past by insisting that the event be made into history again and again. In theory, Christians of all persuasions profess that the cross was done once, for all. Although the Catholic Mass repeats Calvary — and this is the *mysterium fidei* — it does so as oblation representing that one historical immolation, but not repeating it. Atonement, rather, is making one again what sin put asunder, and in Christ God does this on behalf of all who are apart from him, including his enemies, whom he loves despite their mindless and extreme hatred.

Such quality of love, however, interpreted by a ready intellect can often become what is merely expedient. Genius notwithstanding, St Augustine's teaching on just war, for instance, is perilously casuistical. Certainly, Augustine deplores war, and never underestimates its horrors, though allowing that it is sometimes necessary. But he also advises us to take in a spiritual sense Christ's injunctions to 'Resist not evil', and 'turn the other cheek', because Christ did not turn his own cheek when the High Priest slapped him. Soldiers, therefore, may be pacific in 'the inward disposition of their heart', while getting on with disembowelling their enemies, whose spiritual good they serve. The idea that sometimes it 'seems necessary to heal by pain'[8] is in a certain sense true, but in another it is the most dangerously facile of evasions: as for instance, when it was held to be an act of mercy for the Elizabethan soldier Lord Grey to put the Catholic Irish out of their misery by starvation and the sword; or for his contemporaries, the Spaniards in Holland, to display a similar brand of love in the slow fires kindled beneath Protestant heretics.

The spiritual masters, however, as we have seen, insist that the cross mortifies ego – kills the very desire, that is, to impose one's will on another. The principle, 'not I, but Christ in me' depends on willingness to suffer, but to impose no suffering. There is of course never any question of explaining, outside of faith, or avoiding, in any human circumstance, the world's evil. Gautama Buddha, whose whole concern was suffering and the ending of suffering, was empirical in this respect: metaphysical explanations do not alter the facts to be encountered. In some such manner, mysticism in Western tradition insists also on the ascendency of practice over speculation. The saint knows that small acts are of deep importance, and discernment of spirits is the gift of detecting in particulars of word and deed the designs of holiness, the marks of transcendence. True spiritual combat, in short, involves overcoming, in the name of the cross, the desires of an autonomous ego that occludes Spirit. The Preface to Lorenzo Scupoli's *Spiritual Conflict* makes the design clear:

> For our life on earth being a continuall warfare, they [the pages of the book] may serve you to fight against your selves, since that by our Lord you are called and particularly chosen to this no less glorious, than hard conflict. We declare not here how to vanquish cities . . . . but how to get dominion of that kingdome which is within ourselves.
>
> To this spirituall Battel I invite you, and so doth also our Captaine: who for us having left his life upon the crosse, and by his death overcome the world, caleth us to this victory and death of our selves, that we may live eternally with him.[9]

We are to fight, that is, against whatever separates us from God, and Jesus assumed the role of suffering servant to show how, even in extreme affliction, a Son of Man could remain open to transcendence. This he did also in the name of God, so that none out of guilt and fear and desire of dominion should impose the like again: and if the like were imposed, the faithful were to endure as their master, asking forgiveness for their persecutors.

The new design of course was difficult, for it intensified ego-consciousness by stressing individual responsibility and the unique value to God of individuals, while simultaneously indicating that the chief mechanism of evil was ego-assertion, the pride of life. A symbol that calls for others to renounce power over us, and to suffer on our behalf is, after all, conveniently easy to appreciate. It is easy enough, even, to imagine ourselves heroically sacrificed for the general good, if the immolation is not too ignominious. But it is difficult to suffer on behalf of others when the others do not know it is on their behalf, and especially difficult to suffer anonymously, without resentment.

The saints, however, have insisted that only this way, in the end, works. Only a daily taking up of the cross in the sense of refusing to do harm by word or deed, and by accepting with compassion the harm others do to us: in such a way alone is the cross triumphal, for by such means alone can it overcome the vain repetition of itself through the world's Golgothas:

> Compassion is an inward movement of the heart, stirred by pity for the bodily and ghostly griefs of all men. This compassion makes a man suffer with Christ in His passion; for he who is compassionate marks the wherefore of His pains and the way of His resignation; of His love, His wounds, His tenderness . . . . Such a man will also regard with pity the bodily needs of his neighbours, and the manifold sufferings of human nature; seeing men hungry, thirsty, cold, naked, sick, poor, and abject; the manifold oppressions of the poor, the grief caused by loss of kinsmen, friends, goods, honour, peace; all the countless sorrows which befall the nature of man. These things move the just to compassion, so that they share the sorrows of all. But their greatest pain springs from this: that men are so impatient of this suffering, that they lose their reward, and may often earn hell for themselves. Such is the work of compassion and of pity.[10]

Each stage of the body's decay, each moment of unhappiness, is thus a moment of passion to be endured in the body's anonymity, calling finally on faith, in a confrontation which no jejune optimism or palliative distraction or mechanism of ascesis

can deflect. And faith alone declares that the cross finally endured
as abandonment unto death, even in forsakenness that scandalises
theology, is the way beyond separation.

Seen from such a perspective, Trinitarian doctrine assures us
that in some sense God is not impersonal, nor indifferent to
suffering, but rather calls for an end to suffering as for an end to
separation of creatures from their single source of being, itself
beyond being; for an end also to the mechanisms by which we
promulgate further among ourselves the history of suffering and
separation. Indeed, only from such a perspective does Trinitarian
doctrine appear free from the anthropomorphic imperialism of
financial bargaining and neolithic cravings which often
characterise theories of redemption and atonement among the
clerks and scribes. Divorced, that is, from the Son, the Father can
only appear as a tyrannical overlord, and Spirit is forgotten, the
saints ignored, the mystery dissipated among idolatries. It is the
very thing the doctrine itself might serve to prevent, were the way
of the cross practised as the saints have understood it, for the
cross declares God the Son of Man and each man a servant to his
brother, free from infantile subjection to a castigating Father
God.[11]

The Trinity might, then, require of us to know, in spite of all
we cannot know faced with absolute mystery, that God is not
well conceived as the omnipotent superego of some massive
Oedipal imbroglio. Yet the images, broken loose from concepts
and divorced from the mystic vision that preserves God's unity
while calling for a subtle magnificence in the achievement of
character within the world, have often assisted in promoting the
Oedipal neurosis, travesty of the ideal: *corruptio optimi est pessima*.

Freedom to disbelieve, it therefore seems, is at the very least a
precondition for a true understanding of the cross, because otherwise one is faced, in varying degrees, with further devices of
imposition, and, not surprisingly, the Age of Enlightenment in
promoting such an ideal found a means effectively to dissociate
the concerns of religious faith from those of the secular order.
Voltaire's 'écrazez l'infame', though it failed to save poor Jean
Calas[12] from being broken on the wheel, spoke with imperative
clarity: there should be no more atrocity in the name of religion.
Freed, however, to hold God at a distance, the mind must
contend anew with its own appetite for power within the secular
order: though freedom of disbelief does much to prevent the

tyranny of religious persecution, there is no evidence that the new gods of politics and secular ideology have served to stint the destructive rampages of determined egotism.

The spiritual masters talk, therefore, about avoiding the cross, and about the impossibility of avoiding it. The pacifist Gandhiji once stated that it is impossible, while in the body, not to do physical violence. Just so, it is impossible to refrain from violation, in relationships with others, of the ideal, *Christus in me*. Nevertheless, the ideal pursued in a non-violent spirit is central to the *via crucis*, and to whatever of value it teaches. The cross, on the one hand, is neither a brute event (for one cannot communicate the experience of utter forsakenness), nor, on the other hand, a metaphysical sign (life and human suffering are not abstract). The claims of time and eternity are instead to find reconciliation affirming God in the synthesis. Not surprisingly, at various times in Christian history the balance has weighed to one side or the other, but some sense of the symbol containing both elements has characterised Christianity from the beginning.

Early Christian tombs, for instance, were sometimes decorated with butterflies to suggest the resurrected soul, the flight of spirit from the cocoon of a corpse, the body of this death. In Greek, *psyche* meant soul and butterfly together, and the double sense was taken up by those who saw in the grave a hope of eternal life. Christ's charity had likewise shown itself *amor cruciatus*, and so in the world it would remain, the cross a prelude to resurrection.

To the Greeks such a thing was foolishness: the earliest surviving representation of the suffering Jesus is a second-century graffito showing an ass on the cross, with the words 'Alexamenos worships his God'. The cartoon is probably what it seems; a comic denigration by some pagan wag of the new cult of dupes, a mockery of the asses for whom, as the learned Celsus complained also in the second century, Christianity seemed attractive because it was a religion for weaklings. Yet as Celsus also knew, Christian apology was distractingly supple: the magician Jesus, who had learned necromancy in Egypt, as rumour had it, taught his people by a consummate art of shape-shifting to draw their strength everywhere from force used against them. If the Alexamenos graffito were done by a pagan, he was soon, indeed, hoist with his own petard, for the effigy bore a meaning Christians had learned to endure, even welcome.

No believer certainly should be upset by being called a fool (except perhaps by another believer, and St Matthew had already warned against that), for did the Christian not accept his cross of mortal suffering as the means to life and the very sign of faith? Did he not put butterflies on his tombstones? And St Paul after all had told us we should want to be fools, *stulti propter Christum* (1 Cor.: 4, 10).

The shocking necessity of welcoming passion unto death was not, therefore, overlooked in the early Christian centuries, but while the church still harboured expectations of an imminent second coming, and when persecutions against it were harsh, the faithful did not have much cause to make of the cross a special reminder that life was hard. At Rome martyrs burned for emperor and believer alike as candles of the lord. What fools to Nero the Christians must have seemed; what a madman he to them. Yet the more postponed Christ's second coming, the more self-conscious grew the act of belief, in part resignation just to waiting things out. Consequently, during the subsequent millennium the cross became a favourite object of devotion: *memento mori* and injunction to penitence, symbol of love triumphant in the world, and of faith itself enduring patiently. Still, the insight of the early masons remained firm, and the cross was not remade for worship without its *psyche*, the butterfly: God's human suffering remained subordinate to the heavenly glory it intimated. Thus the eleventh-century cross of Lothair, wrought in gold filigree on cloisonné enamel, mounted on a carved rock crystal and featuring an antique cameo of Augustus, represents an eternally regal splendour as well as a physical maiming. We imagine, now, dimly, how this jewel might have caught up the light of votive candles into a symbolic brilliance made actual by faith, inducing upon the brute fact of the transom a change by which death's instruments were made glorious.

An iconographic programme widespread throughout the Middle Ages and early Renaissance shows very well the seriousness and range of such high symbolism. An example is Giovanni Montano's fresco at Bologna, dated 1470, which shows Christ on a cross from the extremities of which grow human arms. The arm on Christ's left wields a sword which strikes at a woman, blindfold and riding on a donkey. The arm on the right places a crown on the head of a woman who bears a chalice into which pours blood from the side wound. The arm beneath wields a hammer which pounds on the gates of hellmouth, while that above opens the gates of Jerusalem with a key.

Dextra and *sinistra* the horizontals tell about history, and how the cross offers release from whatever bondage accompanies a dispensation characterised by legalism and animal sacrifice, in contrast to the blessed *ecclesia* on the right. The verticals tell of eternity, and how the gates of heaven are unlocked and Satan's gains are forfeited. Although the depiction in certain respects lacks subtlety, its main themes are plain: the cross is temporal and trans-temporal, triumphal and penitential, and the more we ponder, the more elusive becomes that intersection, sign of a living faith, a history and a redemption.

With the Renaissance and Reformation, formalised depictions of the triumphal cross yielded to more dramatic representations. These followed a line of development initiated especially by Franciscan devotional practice during the late Middle Ages, and intensified as the act of individual faith itself became a special preoccupation. For Protestants, the Spirit shed its light secretly within, and Catholics at first compensated by giving to the hidden designs of Spirit desperate injections of concreteness. Suffering became more than ever the focus of a curiosity bent on rendering large not so much the glory of the cross as the actual torment: Caravaggio's lurid squalours, Grunewald's flayed hank. As Protestants smashed crucifixes, Catholics rendered theirs unbearably palpable. The puritan John Milton could never write on the passion, though he tried in a youthful, unfinished poem, concluding that the subject was beyond his years. But he never came back to it, even when he later wrote the greatest Christian poetry of his times: the important religious theme for Milton had become temptation, not crucifixion. On the other hand, Milton's contemporary, the Catholic Crashaw, made of the cross something shocking and sensual. Swooning Magdalenes lick the mouths and eyes of Christ's wounds in erotic ardour, as tears fall like pearls and blood like rubies, until in a daze of interpenetrating substances the mind surrenders to the rapture of the cosmic ocean in which fleshly contours are absorbed. It is as if by the end of the seventeenth century the ship of the cross had foundered and left Milton and Crashaw clinging to separate spars – Milton the horizontal and historical; Crashaw the vertical, transcendent mystery.

In the main, the following period of Enlightenment contrived to abandon this *navis crucis*, effectively replacing in conventional piety the crucified God by the more pleasant conception of the divinity as intelligent Designer. Yet the cross did not lose its power as a symbol of interior life, and to Blake and the Romantics, the paradox of polarised energies held in fructifying tension became in relation to the challenge of human creativity, an enduring, even central, preoccupation. The suffering to be borne now in hope of producing the beautiful butterfly was that of imagination itself, and from the tensions within a suffering human mind issued the immortal spirit of art.

Today, we recognise a certain epistemological toughness in literary discussions of such symbols as the cross, together with a tacit, post-Romantic assumption among writers in the line, say, from Dostoevsky to Beckett, that works of imagination are insufficient to absorb violence into easy faith in transcendent reality. W. H. Auden catches the sense of this modern mood:

> The Christian faith is always a scandal to the imagination and reason of the flesh, but the particular aspect which seems most scandalous depends upon the prevailing mentality of a period or a culture. Thus, to both the gnostics of the fourth century and the liberal humanists of the eighteenth, the Cross was an offense, but for quite different reasons. The gnostic said: 'Christ was the Son of God, therefore He cannot have been physically crucified. The Crucifixion was an illusion.' The liberal humanist said: 'Christ was physically crucified, therefore He cannot have been the Son of God. His claim was a delusion.' In our own day, the stumbling block is again different. I think most Christians will find themselves in understanding sympathy with Simone Weil's difficulty: 'If the Gospels omitted all mention of Christ's resurrection, faith would be easier for me. The Cross by itself suffices me.'[13]

Yet the shortcomings of a literary modernism caught between disbelief and disembodied style should not encourage us to hanker for past times when an imputed 'real meaning' of symbols seemed to be embraced more fully and wholeheartedly. Those Christian ages devoted to faith in the redemptive suffering of Calvary were themselves actively intolerant. Crusaders marched beneath the sign of their crosses, reassured that, compared to the innocent redeemer's suffering, the small pains of less sensitive (because less perfect) ordinary flesh were scarcely considerable. The suffering of Christ in consequence managed to unleash its own immeasurable deluge of recrimination, while the eye of a conscience transformed by high-mindedness proclaimed spiritual glory for the successful swords of its partisan warriors. So the French barons who, in the year 1200, sent their envoys to the Doge of Venice, allowed themselves amply to reason that for their Fourth Crusade they were taking the cross to avenge the shame done on Jesus Christ. To this the Doge, Enrico Dandolo, replied that for the love of God he would quickly add to the fleet fifty of his own armed galleys, making that immediately conditional on an even share in the takings by land or sea.

In the ducal palace in Venice still hangs a portrait of Enrico. He appears almost entirely concealed in a carapace of stiff drapery which he holds to himself about his vast middle, like armour, so that only his hands protrude. He wears the bulbous Doge's hat, and from his left hand floats a banner, tightly circling his body and bearing the inscription 'Lord of half and a quarter of the whole Roman Empire'. Against his stylised clothing the head is realistic, with a massive skull suggesting the physical strength we feel in the volume under the drapery. The mouth is tiny, an exaggerated cupid-bow caught between simper and sneer. The high brow-bones give his eyes some baleful earnestness and the cast of a Timurid cruelty. To the innocent eye there is an extraordinary sense of coarse energy which appeal to convention will scarcely explain away, of elemental man garbed in official dress, and in the tight circles of the draperies, the banner, the hat, and the right arm clutching his own middle, an intense self-centredness.

This man, in the portrait so robust, when he replied to the barons that he would be glad to take on their crusade was in fact over ninety years old and almost blind. He had lost his eyesight in Constantinople some thirty years earlier, perhaps in an accident, or perhaps by torture. At any rate, he hated the golden city with all the enormous energies pent up under that official regalia and harboured through his quarter-century of blindness. His pleasure in leading the crusade would thus have a good deal to do with his plan of attack: he would go against Islam by way first of Zara in the Adriatic and then, Constantinople. In each case he would seek cause to reduce these Christian allies to Venetian fealty before proceeding against the common foe, and in each case he would find the cause he sought.

So in 1201, amid an hysteria of tears among a vast congregation in St Mark's, the Doge announced that he would take up his cross. The sign was stitched for him on a great cotton hat, boldly, because he wished all to see it. Almost one hundred years old and nearly blind, with a great crossed hat and his lifetime's habit of huge physical energy concentrated into one last fling of recrimination against the old enemy of Christendom, Enrico led his knights of the cross. Ironically, his rampage ended in so destroying the unity of Byzantium as to open it up soon after to the very conquest by Islam which the Christian armies had, theoretically, set out to prevent. It was done, as the French Barons had put it, for the love of Jesus. Yet if any sin may be named as the transgression against which Jesus gave his coldest warning, it is this assumption of the paraclete's wisdom in taking up the cross to force it on another. What more to exacerbate the enormity, save that the favourite haunt of such misconceit has seemed to remain the court of orthodoxy itself.

The cross in all this has had something of the certainty of unpleasant fact, and for the butterfly we have reserved the elusiveness of Spirit, recorded for history especially in the lives of the saints. But the scandal of the cross remains, for time-enclosed humanity, a perpetual challenge: there is, we are told, a species of butterfly which when it emerges from the pupa state discharges during the first flight some drops of a red fluid. In some instances where their numbers have been considerable these butterflies have produced the appearance of '"a shower of blood" as this natural phenomenon is sometimes called'. The shower, W. J. Holland[14] goes on to say, is also known as the 'red rain', and it has seemed to ancient historians and to poets and to multitudes of ordinary observers that butterflies bleed in their transformation. Ovid mentions it, and so does Livy, and in Stow's *Annales of England* we are told that tempest and desolation followed such a red rain in the year 766 BC. In another account, 'In the time of Brithricus (AD 786), it rayned blood, which falling on men's clothes, appeared like crosses', so that people were astonished. But in the year 1296 the same thing happened in Frankfurt when the butterflies bled and their crosses marked men and buildings and earth. In this case, the historian tells us, 'spots of blood led to a massacre of the Jews' of the town of Frankfurt, 'in which ten thousand of these unhappy descendants of Abraham lost their lives'.

The portent of red rain might fire imagination to accept the bleeding cross first of all, each to his own, hoping, as did those early masons, that a glorified *psyche*, gift of the Spirit, would follow upon mortification. On the contrary, the desire to persecute arose because the Jews were supposed to have spilt the blood, and so the blood, not the butterfly, usurped imagination with a lust simply for expiation which all too conveniently found a target. The cross thus remains with us, as Thomas à Kempis says, calling for our constant self-correction and vigilant discrimination, an art of being both clear and subtle in representing to ourselves the wellsprings of prejudice and motivation. Here, then, in conclusion, is a poem which puts some of these issues dramatically before us with the force and complexity characteristic of great literature:

> Spit in my face yee Jewes, and pierce my side,
> Buffet, and scoffe, scourge, and crucifie mee,
> For I have sinn'd and sinn'd and onely hee,
> Who could do no iniquitie, hath dyed:
> But by my death can not be satisfied
> My sinnes, which passe the Jewes impiety:
> They kill'd once an inglorious man, but I
> Crucifie him daily, being now glorified.
> Oh let mee then, his strange love still admire:
> Kings pardon, but he bore our punishment.
> And Jacob came cloth'd in vile harsh attire
> But to supplant, and with gainfull intent;
> God cloth'd himselfe in vile mans flesh, that so
> Hee might be weake enough to suffer woe.[15]

This is a typical seventeenth-century devotional poem, reconstructing the event both in the speaker's and in the reader's imagination, so that both engage, at different historical times, the continuing challenge offered by the crucifixion. Can we accept for ourselves, and as submissively as Christ, some such lonely suffering without panic-stricken reactions of recrimination and evasion? Also, the poem expresses the turbulence of a man coming to realise the paradox, partly in answer to this question and partly in relation to his own sinfulness, of God's redemptive action, his 'strange love'.

Structurally, the sonnet may be divided into a three-part meditation based on an Ignatian model, adapted by Donne for his Protestant purposes.[16] There are three quatrains: the first, evoking the scene of crucifixion, is the traditional *compositio loci*, the composition of place which uses especially the power of memory. In this section, Donne's speaker pictures himself actually on the cross. The second quatrain brings understanding to bear on what memory has presented as phantasm. The activity of memory and understanding in the octave then contrasts the sestet which resolves the poem in a traditional colloquy or prayer, representing will, the human mind's third faculty. Such a meditation, clearly, is based on a particular view of what the human mind is, whenever it thinks about divine things, at whatever time in history. Its structure shows forth, by analogy, the eternally dynamic form of the mind's source and origin, the Trinity.

The poem also especially dramatises the 'I' in process of discovering, before the cross, the central importance of mortification, and its own radical impotence to overcome separation from God. The first-personal pronoun is conspicuous: 'my face', 'my side', 'mee', 'I', 'my death', 'my sinnes'. Also, the fact that this 'I' learns something makes the distinction between poet and speaker very important. Indeed, the poet deliberately has his speaker assume a false perspective, then to discover that the arrogance causing him to blame others, the egotistical desire, that is, to usurp divine privilege, constitutes, not an acceptance of the message of the cross, but the deepest complicity with those responsible for crucifixions: 'I/Crucifie him daily'.

But we do less than justice to the poem if we fail to sense the *dangerous closeness* of the temptation to blame others, and the frankness with which one such prejudice is here thrust before us: 'Spit in my face, ye Jewes'. If the speaker did not have to struggle against such recrimination within himself there would of course be no poem. Is it not, then, already a reproof of Christian devotion to this terrifying sign of the cross that it stimulates such recrimination so readily? The answer must be yes, in so far as a weight of responsibility for right understanding and right behaviour seems to be placed on human shoulders too weak to carry it. Yet some such challenge as the cross seems inevitable if man is to come to terms with the root paradox of his autonomy and dependence, his self-consciousness and knowledge of death, the midden of his repressed fear, thwarted egotism, and personal instability, the entire mechanism of ego's insecurity expressed as craving for expiation.

The mystics, whose lives attempt truly to follow a way of the cross, know that such a way is discovered only through the care and self-scrutiny of which Donne's poem gives a sense, and they conclude, like him, that resignation to the power of Another in faith is the single means of human salvation. Otherwise, they remain with Donne's speaker in the middle, analytical section of the poem which shows that the paradox of the human situation is heightened but not resolved by analysis. The 'strange love' to which the poem's speaker looks for release is not itself available to the poem's images, and remains mysterious. At the end, he is left waiting on it, and the imagery rather presents the tension of faith that precedes contemplation.

The Doge of Venice in an age of faith refused to act as theory enjoined; John Donne, in an age of doubt affirmed in theory what faith might mean. In an age of disbelief and in face of the facts no theory can help, Simone Weil also discovered the cross. The inexplicable savagery of human affliction, she writes, is a surprising thing, but God has 'created things capable of love from all possible distances. Because no other could do it, he himself went to the greatest possible distance, the infinite distance. This infinite distance between God and God, this supreme tearing apart, this agony beyond all others, this marvel of love, is the crucifixion'. We share in this cross by accepting affliction and the fact of our separation from God. 'This distance is only separation, however, for those who love . . . . This is the only possibility of perfection for us on earth. That is why the cross is our only hope.' In accepting it, we allow ourselves subject to the blind mechanisms of material nature, choosing only the openness possible in love: 'The man to whom such a thing happens has no part in the operation. He struggles like a butterfly pinned alive into an album'.[17]

TEXTS WITHOUT COMMENT
5 THE CROSS

THE CROSS AND ITS PASSING

1. Learn, children, it cannot be otherwise; though we try to
   turn it as we may, we must always bear a Cross.
   > John Tauler (c. 1300–61), Sermon,
   > 'On the Exaltation of the Holy Cross'

2. The mount Calvarie is the mount of Lovers. All love that
   begins not from our Saviours Passion, is frivolous, and
   dangerous. Accursed is death without the Love of our
   Saviour. Accursed is Love, without the death of our
   Saviour. Love and death are so mingled in the passion of our
   Saviour, that one cannot have the one in his heart without
   the other.
   > François de Sales (1567–1622),
   > *Treatise of the Love of God*, XII, 13, 3

3. It is as if one were to see his native land at a distance, and the
   sea intervening; he sees whither he would go, but he has not
   the means of going. So we desire to arrive at that our
   stability where that which is, is, because this alone always is
   as it is: the sea of this world interrupts our course, even
   although already we see whither we go; for many do not
   even see whither they go. That there might be a way by
   which we could go, He has come from Him to whom we
   wished to go. And what has He done? He has appointed a
   tree by which we may cross the sea. For no one is able to
   cross the sea of this world, unless borne by the cross of
   Christ. Even he who is of weak eyesight sometimes
   embraces this cross; and he who does not see from afar
   whither he goes, let him not depart from it, and it will carry
   him over.
   > Augustine of Hippo (354–430),
   > *Homilies on the Gospel of John*, II, 2

4. Let no one assume that he can get rid of the cross without
   getting rid of God.
   > Rulman Merswin (c. 1310–82),
   > *Book of the Nine Rocks*

5. Yes! I do think all kinds of pain and struggle and all un-easy things done with effort, are or can be what I mean by the Way of the Cross. All people who live honestly, intensely and sincerely are treading it in spite of themselves: but it is better to know what one is about. I suppose taken alone it *does* seem rather an austere view of the universe: but I am sick of the feather-bed and dry champagne type of religion, aren't you? *That* is not 'having life more abundantly' anyhow. And surely when it is patent that we are all being kept on the drive (unless we deliberately stagnate) and the whole world and all in it is kept on the drive, and that we are forced to spend our lives and use our energies in humiliating ugly sorts of ways, it is a source of exaltation not of melancholy to know that in this too we are accompanying the Spirit of Christ.

Evelyn Underhill (1875–1941),
Letters, to M.R., 1 Oct 1909

6. Thou shouldst seek all thy rest in me, shouldst willingly suffer wrong from others, desire contempt, mortify thy passions, and die to all thy lusts. Such is the first lesson in the school of wisdom, which is to be read in the open, distended book of My crucified body. And consider and see, whether, if any one in all this world were to do his utmost, he could yet be to Me what I am to him?

Henry Suso (c. 1295–1365),
Little Book of Eternal Wisdom, III

7. Whatever man or woman weeneth to come to contemplation without many such sweet meditations beforehand of their own wretchedness, the passion, the kindness, the great goodness and the worthiness of God, surely he shall err and fail of his purpose. And yet, a man or woman that hath long time been practised in these meditations, must nevertheless leave them, and put them and hold them far down under the cloud of forgetting, if ever he shall pierce the cloud of unknowing betwixt him and his God.

The Cloud of Unknowing (late 14th C.), Ch. 7

8. For as long as He was with them they loved Him much, but it was fleshly in His manhood; and therefore it was speedful to them that He should withdraw the bodily form from their sight, that the Holy Ghost might come to them and teach them to love Him and know Him more ghostly, as He did

on the day of Pentecost. Right so is it speedful to some that our Lord withdraw a little the bodily and fleshly likeness from the eye of the soul, that the heart might be set and fixed more busily in ghostly desire and seeking of His godhead.

Walter Hilton (–1396),
Scale of Perfection, I, 36

9. And surely to tye the Soule generally in all Recollections to a particular curious reflexion on the Circumstances belonging to our Lords Passion, would be as if one should oblige a person that can reade perfectly, and with one glance of his eye joyne a whole sentence together, to make an expresse and distinct Reflexion on each letter, syllable and word: Such a framing and multiplying of Images would only serve to obscure the mind and coole the Affections. Well may such Devout Soules out of time of Prayer, in Reading or discoursing admit such Images, and receive benefit by them in future Recollections. But when they actually pray, then to be forced to stop and restraine the will from melting into Divine Love, or from sacrificing herselfe to God by Perfect Resignation etc, till she have passed through her former imperfect Method of Imaginative Meditation, is all one as to forbid Soules to unite themselves in Spirit to the Divinity.

Augustine Baker (1575–1641),
Sancta Sophia, Treatise III, 125–6

10. Secondly, a Soul looseth the sight of Christ in the last Tryals, because God at that time takes away from the Soul the possession and reflected knowledge of all that is good in her, to purifie her from all self-interest. In this state of unvoluntary darknes and trouble, the Soul looses no more the sight of Christ than of God. But all these losses are but in appearance and transient.

François Fenelon (1651–1715),
Maxims of the Saints, V, 107

11. The Lover lay in the bed of love: his sheets were of joy, his coverlet was of griefs, his pillow of tears. And none knew if the fabric of the pillow was that of the sheets or of the coverlet.

Ramon Lull (1235–1316),
The Book of the Lover and the Beloved, 127

12. The Lover drank deeply of the wine of memory, understanding and love for his Beloved. And that wine the

Beloved made bitter with His Lover's tears.
Ramon Lull (1235–1316),
The Book of the Lover and the Beloved, 363

PERSONS IN GOD

13. Let us die, then, and pass over into the darkness; let us silence every care, every craving, every dream; with Christ crucified, let us pass out of this world to the Father.

Bonaventure (1221–74),
The Journey of the Mind to God, VII, 6

14. The enlightened man shall also mark and behold the attributes of the Father in the Godhead: how He is omnipotent Power and Might, Creator, Mover, Preserver, Beginning and End, the Origin and Being of all creatures. This the rill of grace shows to the enlightened reason in its radiance. It also shows the attributes of the Eternal Word: abysmal Wisdom and Truth, Pattern of all creatures and all life, Eternal and unchanging Rule, Seeing all things and Seeing Through all things, none of which is hidden from Him; Transillumination and Enlightenment of all saints in heaven and on earth, according to the merits of each. And even as this rill of radiance shows the distinctions between many things, so it also shows to the enlightened reason the attributes of the Holy Ghost: incomprehensible Love and Generosity, Compassion and Mercy, infinite Faithfulness and Benevolence, inconceivable Greatness, outpouring Richness, a limitless Goodness drenching through all heavenly spirits with delight, a Flame of Fire which burns all things together in the Unity, a flowing Fountain, rich in all savours, according to the desire of each; the Preparation of all saints for their eternal bliss and their entrance therein, an Embrace and Penetration of the Father, the Son, and all saints in fruitive Unity. All this is observed and beheld without differentiation or division in the simple Nature of the Godhead.

John of Ruysbroeck (1293–1381),
Adornment of the Spiritual Marriage, Ch. XXXVII

15. But in the Trinity which is God, those who are three are very truly one; and they are not three gods but one God of

one nature and the same essence. And predication of one essence implies perfect unity. Therefore when someone asks about the Father, the Son, and the Holy Spirit, whether they are three and what the three are, on the authority of the Lord and in accordance with the reasoning of faith, there is no better answer nor one closer to the truth than that they are one.

William of St Thierry (1085–1148),
Enigma of Faith, 31

16. Thus the Unity is ever drawing to itself and inviting to itself everything that has been born of It, either by nature or by grace. And therefore, too, such enlightened men are, with a free spirit, lifted up above reason into a bare and imageless vision, wherein lives the eternal indrawing summons of the Divine Unity; and, with an imageless and bare understanding, they pass through all works, and all exercises, and all things, until they reach the summit of their spirits. There, their bare understanding is drenched through by the Eternal Brightness, even as the air is drenched through by the sunshine. And the bare, uplifed will is transformed and drenched through by abysmal love, even as iron is by fire. And the bare, uplifted memory feels itself enwrapped and established in an abysmal Absence of Image.

John of Ruysbroeck (1293–1381),
The Book of Supreme Truth, Ch. XI

17. And – that we turn again to the highest things, and end our denyings at things most high – we say that he hath no virtue, nor he is virtue, nor light, nor he liveth, nor he is life, nor he is substance, nor age, nor time, nor there is any understandable touching of him, nor he is knowledge, nor truth, nor kingdom, nor wisdom, nor one, nor unity, nor Godhead or goodness; nor he is spirit, as we understand spirit; nor sonhood, nor fatherhood, nor any other thing known by us or by any that be; nor he is anything of not-being things, nor anything of being things; nor any of those things that be, know him as he is; nor he knoweth those things that be as they be in themselves, but as they be in him.

Dionise Hid Divinite (late 14th C.), Ch. 5

COMBAT AND TOLERATION

18. Another device there is: prove thou if thou wilt. When thou feelest that thou mayest in nowise put them down, cower then down under them as a caitiff and a coward overcome in battle, and think that it is but folly to strive any longer with them; and therefore thou yieldest thyself to God in the hands of thine enemies. And feel then thyself as though thou wert overcome for ever. Take good heed of this device, I pray thee; for I think that in the proof of this device thou shouldst melt all to water. And surely, I think, if this device be truly conceived, it is nought else but a true knowing and a feeling of thyself as thou art, a wretch and a filthy thing, far worse than nought: the which knowing and feeling is meekness. And this meekness meriteth to have God himself mightily descending, to venge thee of thine enemies, so as to take thee up and cherishingly dry thy ghostly eyes, as the father doth his child that is on the point to perish under the mouths of wild swine or mad biting bears.

The Cloud of Unknowing (late 14th C.), Ch. 32

19. Every war fought between us and the impure spirits is engaged in for no other cause than that of spiritual prayer. This is an activity that is intolerable to them, they find it so hostile and oppressive. To us, on the other hand, it is both pleasant in the highest degree and spiritually profitable.

Evagrius Ponticus (345–99),
Chapters on Prayer, 49

20. *Eternal Wisdom.* – No one can attain divine exaltation or singular sweetness except by passing through the image of My human abasement and bitterness. The higher one climbs without passing through My humanity, the deeper one falls. My humanity is the way one must go, My Passion the gate through which one must penetrate, to arrive at that which thou seekest. Therefore, lay aside thy faint-heartedness, and enter with Me the lists of knightly resolve: for, indeed, softness beseems not the servant when his master stands ready in warlike boldness. I will put thee on My coat of mail, for My entire Passion must thou suffer over again according to thy strength.

Henry Suso (c. 1295–1365),
Little Book of Eternal Wisdom, II

21. Let Christ crucified alone be enough for you; with Him suffer, with Him take your rest, never rest nor suffer without Him; striving with all your might to rid yourself of all selfish affections and inclinations in the annihilation of self.

John of the Cross (1542–91),
Spiritual Maxims, 6

22. These Bloodthirsty Expeditions were called an holy War, because it was a fighting for the holy Land; they were called also a Croisade, because Crosses and Crucifixes made the greatest Glitter among the sharpened Instruments of human Murder. – Thus under the Banner of the Cross went forth an Army of Church Wolves, to destroy the Lives of those, whom the Lamb of God died on the Cross to save. The Light which broke out at the Reformation, abhorred the bloody superstitious Zeal of these Catholic Heroes. – But (N.B.) what followed from this new risen, reforming Light, what came forth instead of these holy Croisades? Why Wars, if possible, still more diabolical. – Christian Kingdoms with bloodthirsty Piety, destroying, devouring, and burning one another, for the Sake of That which was called Popery, and That which was called Protestantism. Now who can help seeing, that Satan, the Prince of the Powers of Darkness, had here a much greater Triumph over Christendom, than in all holy Wars and Croisades that went before? For all that was then done, by such high-spirited Fighters for old Jerusalem's Earth, could not be said to be so much done against Gospel-Light, because not one in a Thousand of those holy Warriors were allowed to see what was in the Gospel. But now, with the Gospel opened in everyone's Hands, Papists and Protestants make open War against every Divine Virtue that belonged to Christ, or that can unite them with that Lamb of God, that taketh away the Sins of the World: – I say against every Divine, redeeming Virtue of the Lamb of God, for these are the Enemies which Christian War conquers. For there is not a Virtue of Gospel-goodness, but has its Death-blow from it.

William Law (1686–1761),
Address to the Clergy

23. If they will thus persecute me through all Christendom, I shall be obliged to go among the Turks, and I believe they will be better dispos'd to receive the Truths of God, than the

Christians are; and by this Means, you may as yet come to Jerusalem.

Antoinette Bourignon (1616–80),
Letters, XIX, 6

24. Why do I despise him that is short of me, not knowing but that he may not be below me? Allow him to be a foot of the Body, rather than exclude him. In the Body if it fare ill with any Member, the whole resents it, and is sympathetically affected therewith.

Benjamin Whichcote (1609–83),
Select Notions, 'Phil. III, xv', 11

25. See that you do not intermeddle in the affairs of other people, nor discuss them in your own thoughts; for perhaps you will not be able to fulfil your own task.

John of the Cross (1542–91),
Spiritual Maxims, 124

26. If religion forbids all instances of revenge without any exception, it is because all revenge is of the nature of poison; and though we do not take so much as to put an end to life, yet if we take any at all, it corrupts the whole mass of blood, and makes it difficult to be restored to our former health.

If religion commands an universal charity, to love our neighbour as ourselves, to forgive and pray for all our enemies without any reserve; it is because all degrees of love are degrees of happiness, that strengthen and support the divine life of the soul and are as necessary to its health and happiness, as proper food is necessary to the health and happiness of the body.

William Law (1686–1761),
A Serious Call, Ch. XI

27. Behold! thou blind Man, I will demonstrate this to thee thus: Go into a Meadow, there thou seest several Sorts of Herbs, and Flowers; thou seest some that are bitter, some tart, sweet, sour, white, yellow, red, blue, green; and many various Sorts.

Do they not all grow out of the Earth? Do they not stand one by another? Does the one grudge the beauteous Form of the other?

But if one among them lifts up itself too high in its Growth, and so withers, because it has not Sap enough, how can the Earth help it? Does it not afford its Sap to that as well as to the other?

But if Thorns grow among them, and the Mower comes to reap his Crop, he cuts them down together, but he casts out the Thorns, and they are to be burnt in the Fire; but the various Flowers and good Crop he gathers, and causes it to be brought into his Barn.

Thus it is also with Men, there are Diversities of Gifts and Accomplishments, Endowments, or Aptitudes; one it may be is much lighter or brighter in God than another; but all the while they do not wither in the Spirit, they are not rejectible; but when the Spirit withers, then that is good and useful for Nothing but for Fewel, and is only as Wood for the Fire.

But if the Turks be of an astringent Quality, and the Heathens of a bitter, what is that to thee? Is the Light become shining in the astringent and bitter Qualities? then it gives Light also.

But thou art generated in the Heat, where the Light rises up in the sweet Spring or Fountain-Water; have a Care lest the Heat burn thee; it is Time, thou shouldst do well to quench that.

Jacob Boehme (1575–1624),
Aurora, 2, 65–71

28. Let us look at our own faults, and not at other persons'. People who are extremely correct themselves are often shocked at everything they see; however, we might often learn a great deal that is essential from the very persons whom we censure. Our exterior comportment and manners may be better – this is well enough, but not of the first importance. We ought not to insist on every one's following in our footsteps, nor to take upon ourselves to give instructions in spirituality when perhaps, we do not even know what it is.

Teresa of Avila (1515–82),
Interior Castle, Third Mansion, II, 19

29. Another thing is necessary for thee to arrive at this union and purity, namely, that thou shouldest never judge the will of man in anything that thou mayest see done or said by any creature whatsoever, either to thyself or to others. My will alone shouldst thou consider, both in them and in thyself. And, if thou shouldest see evident sins or defects, draw out

of those thorns the rose, that is to say, offer them to Me, with holy compassion.

Catherine of Siena (1347–80),
The Dialgue, 'A Treatise of Prayer', C

30. But it is a clear sign of a soul that is not yet thoroughly purged from the dregs of sin, not to sorrow with a feeling of pity at the offences of others, but to keep to the rigid censure of the judge: for how will he be able to obtain perfection of heart, who is without that by which, as the Apostle has pointed out, the full requirements of the law can be fulfilled, saying: 'Bear one another's burdens and so fulfil the law of Christ.'

John Cassian (c. 360–435),
Conferences, XI, 10

CHAPTER SIX
The Way

It seems we cannot be still and know without first launching out along some path, and, for the literature and practice of mysticism, taking a direction accompanies the act of faith in which knowledge begins. But progress in mystical prayer is not linear and straightforward: it involves a deepening experience of the centre, the point of departure which is also the point of understanding.

Because the depths of human experience are best communicated as a quality of style (the embodiment, as it were, of surface meaning), there are various descriptions of the life of prayer, instructing us to follow not just a set of directions but a set of attitudes and a manner of behaviour. Style best expresses the particular strangeness and beauty of experience, imparting a distinctive quality which, mystics tell us, we should value in life, and which, critics advise, we should appreciate in literature. It would be difficult, for instance, to describe differences between Edmund Spenser's story of Redcrosse Knight and John Bunyan's similar story of Christian's journey to the Heavenly City in terms of creed alone. We respond rather to the peculiar bias and pattern of a poetic voice intent on giving a personal account of the trials and delights which such a journey entails. Bunyan's pilgrim, unlike Spenser's, feels continually the problem of taking directions and of finding his way. The entire story has Christian repeatedly renew a mysterious impulse which caused him at the outset to leave his wife and children and to head off in bewilderment, except concerning the single point that an interior light, which he could not command, was to be his guide. Bunyan thus draws attention to the mystery within; Christian follows one highly particular course to Jerusalem, and his adventures are less important for the progress they suggest along a pre-existent route which all men can follow, than for their insistence on the continuing mystery of interior illumination by which God leads him (and, consequently, each of us) through any diversity of circumstances.

Redcrosse Knight encounters the mystery less self-consciously, and his adventures are, for him, just that: adventures. They have for the reader, however, a pattern which the knight himself does not see. Redcrosse is, after all, holiness – an interior state which *we* can appreciate by discovering its design or general significance, but which *he* embodies. Yet Spenser's landscapes of forests and plains and seashore suggest that many ways are possible within the pattern, and in this respect *The Faerie Queene* stands in contrast to Bunyan's description of Christian's road, which shows us only one way.[1]

We face, here, not exclusive alternatives, but two distinctive assessments of what is important in finding the path to Jerusalem. Spenser tends initially to stress the objectivity of traditional images and symbols, suggesting that they are reliable guideposts which tell of enduring human truths, even though the highest vision is beyond their reach. Bunyan starts with the fact that each of us journeys alone, waiting on grace, and stresses that conveying the radical subjectivity of such an experience is the main aim of literature. Christian's progress is a series of encounters in which he is repeatedly rescued by divine grace, so that the general pattern of his adventures is much less important than the repeated, inexplicable miracle of God's saving intervention. Yet, for Bunyan, words share in the mystery, and, to his terrified amazement, he discovers himself a potential means of grace for his readers: the Spirit might use his book to show others the way, despite the book's proclamation that each must find his own way.

These two approaches may be taken, broadly, to correspond to the difference between *via affirmativa* and *via negativa*, the ways of affirmation and negation of images. But Spenser and Bunyan also make clear that such separate 'ways' overlap: in Bunyan's pilgrim we recognise situations typical of Christian life and tradition, which remain part of the book's meaning; in Spenser's Redcrosse Knight, we follow the story of a particular, often foolish young man with whom we do not at all points identify. The exponent of *via affirmativa*, in short, if he truly elaborates his position, will end up acknowledging (like Spenser) how images are insufficient, just as his counterpart will discover (like Bunyan) their efficacy. The purest Protestant does not avoid the claim of tradition upon him; the most conservative Catholic cannot deny authenticity to a uniquely personal voice. We are all Protestants with respect to each other, says W. H. Auden sagely, and Catholics with respect to the truth.[2]

One characteristic of great writing on the subject of spiritual progress is, therefore, to take a certain position and to proceed along a definite way, and yet to make of the commitment something infinitely suggestive of realities that lie outside its particular path or trajectory. There is a certain 'roundness' to such writing which is partly fruit of an ability not to identify wisdom literally with any method or sequence of steps or stages, while nonetheless holding that we are creatures of contingency and need to commit ourselves to particular paths of action. 'I am the way, and the truth, and the life' (John, 14:6) said Jesus, suggesting, uncompromisingly, that we follow his way, but indicating that truth and life are his way also, so that it becomes difficult to determine a formula for imitation. And according to the gospel record, Jesus spoke in a manner both commanding and fraught with ambiguities. Orthodoxy has intended, correspondingly, to allow us to find our own way amidst life's perplexities, being imperative about heresy only when there is an exaggeration of some particular truth to a degree that threatens the validity of some other truth that seems equally indispensable. Thus, the tangle of theological argument about Jesus' divine and human nature represents an attempt to avoid what is unacceptable, rather than to prescribe clear answers, and the historical Jesus survives most persuasively as a man who asked us to have faith, like his, accepting the gift of life unto death in such a manner as befits our circumstances and capacities.

But although we are to respect a variety of approaches to God, this does not entail disrespect for generalisation. It suggests, rather, that general directives in the *via mystica* are more like a map than the terrain itself. A guide, or spiritual director, can be useful; if he does not know the highest peaks by experience, he should be an expert map-reader who can advise about directions he cannot himself take. His gift is in discernment of spirits, and he must read the signs with tact and subtlety. According to St Teresa, he is to be prudent, pious, learned and kind. He should have a sound knowledge of tradition, and be able to provide explanations enabling those under his direction to understand, and so come to terms with, experiences which constitute higher levels of prayer.[3] His position, we might say, is analogous to that of the critic attempting to combine learning and sensitivity to appraise the value of poetry, revealing in the process principles of structure and organisation which can become touchstones for the reception of further literature within the tradition. For this task he needs, also, a sense of cultural context, maintaining a balance between knowledge and sympathetic receptivity, combining method and insight to render experience of the Good intelligible. True love, he seems to say, thrives best when there is also love of truth.

The problem of where and how to begin remains, therefore, enigmatically simple, and maps of how we may proceed are incomplete, though not useless. We are asked to begin, and to chart a course, however tentatively. Not many, we are assured, arrive in this life at the Unitive state, but it is pointless to reserve the term 'mysticism' for the few who have such experience even though we must avoid diluting the word so that it describes psyche's everyday activity. Within a diversity of schemes we are, instead, to catch the sense of how a variety of paths converges upon one extraordinary truth of the Father made manifest in the Son, through Spirit.

Attempts to classify historical descriptions[4] of the *via mystica* must soon encounter the particular complexities raised by such considerations, not least because it is impossible to trace back the religious experience of mankind to some original revelation or insight. The problem of origins instead is mirrored and infinitely refracted through the more proximate sources with which history can grapple, and, for Christianity, the most obvious of these, as we have seen, are Hebrew religion and Greek philosophy.

In Judaism, God confronts man in time, though in a manner preserving the divine omnipotence: although Genesis reassures us that we are created in God's image, we are repeatedly called to acknowledge the creator's transcendence in a manner discouraging to doctrines of mystical absorption in which self could be identified with Divinity. Isaiah's vision of the Lord on a high throne, like Ezekiel's of the heavenly chariot, can combine with Hosea's description of Jehova as lover and husband, or the powerful intimacy of the psalms, to suggest a vision of the

Almighty at once transcendent, yet filling the events of time and the hearts of men with his presence.

If the Hebrews described first-hand experiences of God met face to face, the Greeks by contrast developed a vocabulary for dealing with metaphysical problems occasioned by a soul's encounter with Absolute Reality, the Pure Form of being. For Socrates and his great successors, Plato, Aristotle, Plotinus and Proclus, the principal task was to preserve the unity of being without allowing the world of appearances to slip wholly into insignificance. Thus challenged, these thinkers developed a metaphysical system in which things were held more real as they approached the One Source, and less so as they suffered declension and fragmentation in proportion to their material embodiment. Within such a scheme, the human soul or higher reason is held, uniquely, to participate in the divine principle with which its destiny is united, and the way of soul's reunion with its source is described most beautifully by Plotinus, as a progress through a series of grades towards perfection, a scheme which deeply influenced subsequent Christian thought.

It is conventional to notice a special meeting point of the Hebrew and Greek traditions in Philo of Alexandria, a Hellenistic Jew of the first century BC, who wrote commentaries on Genesis and Exodus. Philo supposed that because Greek philosophy was rooted in the Bible therefore the Bible could be made in turn to reveal a 'Platonic' dimension through allegorical reading. But although remarkable in his own right, Philo is also symptomatic of an immense intellectual and spiritual ferment accompanying the confluence of Hebrew and Greek cultures, at the heart of which the New Testament was engendered and its central events enacted. On the one hand, Jesus according to John had promised the Paraclete and had talked in Messianic terms of a second coming and a judgement. On the other, Jesus assured his disciples, in language seductive to Greeks, of his status as *Logos*, existing 'in my Father, and you in me and I in you' (John 14:11–20). St Paul likewise felt and attested the fact of becoming, in some such fashion, a member of Christ's body through Spirit, of being filled by a life higher than his own: 'I live, now not I', he dared to venture, 'but Christ liveth in me' (Gal. 2:20). Paul distinguished also between spiritual children who cannot take solid food, and others who possess the higher knowledge,[5] but gave no detailed classification of ways in which we can progress from one level to the other, insisting simply that love is the criterion of advancement. Beyond this, there is not much systematic exposition of a spiritual path in New Testament writings. The consistency, however, with which Jesus expressed transparency to a Transcendent Will by adjustment of his inner life to its unseen source, was to motivate and enable a diverse witness to membership in his mystical body.

To trace the contours of a typical spiritual progress in Christian terms is, therefore, difficult, for each road to God is, as Bunyan says, unique. But in some sense each tale if well told will reflect a generally recognisable experience in light of which the attempt to define a spiritual Way can grow and develop. Certainly, at the beginnings of Christian tradition the sense of particular people searching out the possibilites of different approaches to God is prominent, and prefaces a subsequent historical movement of slow convergence and consolidation into a tradition.

At the beginning, with the martyrs, for instance, it is hard to tell if ecstasy while facing the beasts was due to anaesthetic terror or supernatural intervention. Such is the case with Perpetua, who found herself wondering aloud about when she was to be gored and tossed, after these dreadful things had in fact been done. By contrast, among the early Fathers who lived also under threat of persecution, the formulation of theories demonstrating how Christians could think like Greeks was in part conciliatory. Such theories suggested that Christians ought not, after all, to be persecuted as promoters of a dangerous, new-fangled ideology, because *gnosis* was their aim, and Stoic asceticism their method. Thus Clement of Alexandria and his pupil Origen describe a Christian gnosticism to which the various efforts of ascetic practice can lead, so that a man's ascent to true knowledge is through 'leaving all hindrances, and despising all matter which distracts him'.[6] Origen developed also a theory of 'spiritual senses', and in a commentary on the *Song of Songs* instituted a tradition, which would find special fulfilment in St Bernard and St John of the Cross, and which described the highest knowledge as a bridal consummation.

When persecution ceased, or abated, the intensities it engendered were soon re-expressed as another kind of martyrdom, the 'white martyrdom' of the hermits and desert-dwellers: Methodius' *Symposium*, the first Christian work on virginity, states plainly that virgins are martyrs. St Athanasius (d. 375), who followed Methodius' principle in his *Letter to the Virgins*, wrote also a *Life of Antony* (c. 357) which became a classic statement of how self-denial and seclusion are a means of restoring that original nature from which we are departed into worldliness. The martyrs' example was thus perpetuated in ascetic practice which, as in Clement and Origen, was to precede *gnosis*. In this respect the example of Antony had a crucial influence on the great Augustine, who records it in *The Confessions*, and through Palladius' (d. before 431) *Lausiac History* and Cassian's (c. 360–435) *Conferences* the sayings of the desert fathers also passed into Western tradition.

It is inviting to detect among patristic writers certain adumbrations of future schemes and stages of the mystical way, but retrospect can easily ignore the tentativeness and variety of these early instructions on the spiritual life. Still, one modification of the predominant binary scheme of *ascesis* and *gnosis* is worth mentioning: the proposal, that is, by Evagrius Ponticus (345–99), a desert monk, to subdivide contemplation, or *gnosis*, into lower and higher forms. Evagrius' consequent threefold division at a later date was associated with a scheme implicit in the writings of Dionysius the Areopagite, distinguishing purgation, illumination and union, to constitute the famous three-fold way of Western mysticism, which found its fullest and most systematic elaboration in the *De Triplici Via* of St Bonaventure.

Evagrius thus helped to give, especially to Eastern monasticism but also to some extent to the West, a plan of contemplative life which married Alexandrian tradition with the Dionysian 'negative way'. For the West, however, before the revival of Dionysian tradition in the twelfth century, desert wisdom was consolidated with patristic tradition in a most influential form, not by Evagrius, but by Cassian, who gave to the 'Benedictine centuries' a form of contemplative theology at once ascetic, clear-headed and intellectual, but not extravagant. Like Augustine, Cassian stressed gradual perfection in the degrees of love under the influence of grace. Augustine, we recall, distinguished between corporeal, spiritual and intellectual vision, and described an ascent through a 'song of degrees' from the multitudinous variety of material creation, towards the One. He also described this ascent in terms of an intensification of love, through initial, progressing and perfect stages. The spirit of Augustine's approach passed, especially through Cassian, to Gregory and Bernard, constituting, according to Cuthbert Butler,[7] the main tradition of Western mysticism.

In the twelfth century this tradition came to a head, and in his controversy with Abelard, St Bernard was already in contention with a new intellectual movement. The major change of emphasis was caused by scholastic philosophy, with its penchant to classify and describe 'ladders of perfection', and also by the rediscovery of Dionysius. Notably in Hugh and Richard of St Victor, the combination of scholastic classification and Dionysian language of 'divine darkness' (for which, scholars have now shown, Dionysius is indebted to Gregory of Nyssa) produced a dynamic account of the life of prayer, not replacing older tradition, but providing new vigour and excitement. As St Bonaventure especially makes clear, by the thirteenth century the Augustine-inspired idea of progress through beginning, developing and perfect charity had combined with Dionysian distinction between purgation, illumination and union to suggest that the Dionysian scheme could be seen also as a series of stages along the way of love.

With the rise of nominalism and the crisis of Renaissance and Reformation, a further efflorescence of mystical writing turned scholastic classification increasingly inward and produced a literature of remarkable subtlety and psychological insight. The brilliant Meister Eckhart (1260–1327), for instance, was a pupil of Albertus Magnus, as was Thomas Aquinas, but in Eckhart Dominican theology and scholastic training subserve a highly individual mystic vision which was to exert widespread influence in Northern Europe. Likewise, devotional poetry found increasingly in handbooks of meditation and manuals of spiritual direction a means of analysing individual spiritual experience according to a variety of schemes and styles catering for a diversity of psychological types. Not surprisingly, one can distinguish, during this period, between schools of thought which gave to mysticism the flavour of particular national cultures. For instance, the fourteenth-century contemplatives, Richard Rolle, the author of the *Cloud of Unknowing*, Walter Hilton, and Dame Julian of Norwich, interpreted European tradition in a manner distinctively English, marked by a practical turn of mind and a kind of Chaucerian energy and charm. Although Rolle's

emotionalism on the surface seems quite different from the
Dionysian theology of the *Cloud*, both authors write with comparable immediacy and the unaffected, idiosyncratic humour
characteristic of the group.

In the Netherlands, a distinctive tradition grew up in the
context of certain pious communities, especially through the
diocese of Liège, which helped to disseminate the teachings of St
Bernard throughout the Low Countries. Consequently, strong
elements of bridal mysticism characterise the Netherlandish
tradition, and John of Ruysbroeck (1293–1381), who founded
the Abbey of Groendaal in 1350, wrote there his best known
work, *The Adornment of the Spiritual Marriage*, subsequently
popularised by his disciple, Henry Herp (d.1477), whence it
influenced the Spanish mystics, as well as the French School. The
Brethren of the Common Life, founded in the Low Countries by
Gerard Groote (1340–84), likewise profoundly influenced the
course of European spirituality through the example of community life stressing an affective, apostolic imitation of Christ,
the most famous account of this ideal being *The Imitation of
Christ*, by Thomas à Kempis.

Spanish tradition is also distinctive, comprising the works of
such as Luis de Granada, John of St Thomas, Peter of Alcantara,
Juan de Valdès, Bernardino Ochino, Ignatius Loyola, and the
famous Carmelites, Teresa of Avila and John of the Cross. Theirs
is a strenuously ecclesial school: St Teresa and St John were
continually concerned with church structure and reform,
submitting themselves repeatedly to examination by ecclesiastical authorities. Ignatius Loyola's keyword was 'obedience',
and, taking up a peculiarly Spanish quality of militant,
heroic spirituality, his followers spearheaded the Counter-
Reformation. There is a special dramatic intensity in Spanish
tradition, as doctrines of illumination, touched by Islamic
influence, contend with a discipline of obedience and abnegation.

The French, though drawing on Spanish and Netherlandish
sources, produced their own *École Française*. Such figures as
Benet of Canfield, Pierre de Bérulle, Mme Acarie, François de
Sales, and Nicolas Malebranche, proposed, as we have seen,
strongly theocentric devotion in response to rising rationalist
fashion, and in contrast to the English, the French tradition tends
towards a distinctive intellectualism.

One inevitable result of such diversification was realised

when, with the advent of religious toleration and secularism, the key question became not how to choose sound means of expressing religious faith, but whether or not to have religious faith at all. The question of 'ways' consequently became highly complicated. Blake was of the opinion that his choice lay in being enslaved to another man's system, or in making his own, and although he made his own, scholars have shown that he did not create without beginning somewhere: without taking a place, that is, in tradition, and using the common language.

Freedom of imagination such as Blake proclaimed, however, has remained important to the story of spiritual writing in the West in modern times, and has, among other effects, made the arbitrariness of some sort of willed commitment painfully clear. Here, for instance, is Henry Thoreau describing his sense of nature's priceless beauty, which he came to appreciate after spending almost two years in solitude in the New England woods, near Walden Pond:

> White Pond and Walden are great crystals on the surface of the earth, Lakes of Light. If they were permanently congealed, and small enough to be clutched, they would, perchance, be carried off by slaves, like precious stones, to adorn the heads of emperors; but being liquid, and ample, and secured to us and our successors forever, we disregard them, and run after the diamond of Kohinoor. They are too pure to have a market value; they contain no muck. How much more beautiful than our lives, how much more transparent than our characters, are they! We never learned meanness of them. How much fairer than the pool before the farmer's door, in which his ducks swim! Hither the clean wild ducks come. Nature has no human inhabitant who appreciates her. The birds with their plumage and their notes are in harmony with the flowers, but what youth or maiden conspires with the wild luxuriant beauty of Nature? She flourishes most alone, far from the towns where they reside. Talk of heaven! ye disgrace earth.[8]

The emphasis on purity and cleanness shows Thoreau's preoccupation with the idea that a disciplined, ascetic existence brings to light nature's higher laws. He has lost himself in the woods, in a sense, to find illumination. But the tone of challenge, even abrasiveness, is just as clear, and we get a further sense that

Thoreau's self-imposed exile is intended not only as a means of finding enlightenment, but of rebuking the less committed who conform unthinkingly to convention. We respond, in this passage, to a shift from cadenced and allusive language ('the diamond of Kohinoor', 'crystals on the surface of the earth'), to something almost vehement ('they contain no muck', 'Talk of heaven! ye disgrace earth'). Gracious speech is not beyond this author's skill, but a kind of downrightness immediately qualifies his use of it, showing us how he sees through it, and how suspicious he is of people who would use elegant conventions simply to mask their indolence and conceal their meanness: 'Nature', after all, 'has no human inhabitant who appreciates her'.

Thoreau thus strikes us first as craggy and individualistic, and is deliberately dogmatic to upbraid us for being otherwise. He can state beautiful truths about man's mystical union with nature – the sense of passing an invisible boundary, as he says elsewhere, and encountering a higher law (p. 343) – but never as a sentimentalist: rather, he remains the self-aware, hard-edged character who despised institutions and refused to pay his taxes. He found his own way, and tells us loudly that it is *his* way. Yet a major fascination for the reader of *Walden* is to discover that Thoreau's individualism does not amount just to isolation. The mixture of self-deprecatory irony, intelligence, humour and learning renders the book a complex witness to the task of finding wholeness in a modern civilisation, in a manner that preserves freedom to choose directions, and which does not veer into indifference or solipsism. There is a sense, even, in which Thoreau *is especially* interested in the farmer's mucky pool, intimating that pure beauty encountered in isolation leans towards sterility. Here, the question of stages along a way, of classifications and schemes, yields almost completely to a kind of guidance which style best communicates. Thoreau warns us against the schematic, but, in so doing, makes clear that we must, nonetheless, be decisive. We must realise that our way is not quite his, but we should appreciate his style, and try to do something comparable on our own account.

Since Thoreau's time, models to imitate have proliferated enormously. In particular, sacred literature of Eastern traditions has disclosed to the West a complexity of ways and means: texts in translation and gurus in person are today a sufficiently obvious fact of life in Western culture. One result is, perhaps, that the power of strangeness by which the East repeatedly has seeded Western imagination is to a degree dissipated by familiarity and commercialism. But the phenomenon nonetheless challenges Western tradition to resist a characteristic tendency to stiffen in its own integument. And yet ecumenism cannot be by way of interior collapse, and the West needs, still, to understand its spiritual history and to reimagine how its characteristic techniques of dividing to conquer, of analysing to control, were developed from a state of mind and language which once knew the life of Spirit more objectively in the world. Non-Western traditions whose emphasis is less on progress than on the timeless Unmanifest can provide insight, as we have suggested earlier, to aid this process, and to prevent an aimless materialism, relying on technique and magical manipulation, from losing all sense of the original mystery.[9] Dr Faustus, we recall, in attempting to deny his spiritual past managed only to reincarnate the old demons in an all-too concrete present. In this respect, genuine mystics condemn not only the obvious excesses of materialism, but advise against procedures which promise the achievement, by adepts, of special powers. Such phenomena as raptures, stigmata, the sense of physical lightness, clairvoyance, auditions, and so on, we are told, are insignificant and should not be sought after. 'I will only warn you', writes St Teresa, 'that, when you learn or hear that God is granting souls these graces, you must never beseech or desire Him to lead you along this road'.[10] Humility and intelligence are rather to remain active in their proper mode, for these best disarm spurious religiosity bent on achieving magical power.

The way lies, therefore, through a tradition combining love of truth with analysis that teaches avoidance of error. Beginnings and ends remain obscure, and one addresses them in the night of faith – itself, in the last analysis, a gift of grace. Along such a way, progress is continually surprising, and corresponds to no clear laws. *Religio*, meanwhile, binds us back to the rule of reason and humane discipline, requiring, by the practice of cult and education, of symbol and rite and doctrine, that in the midst of the splendour we do not forget our place with mankind, to whom we look for support and correction.

Such a synthesis of effects, combining clear teaching with particular insight, and mapping the spiritual way by 'roundness' of style, is realised with distinction in St Teresa's masterpiece, *The Interior Castle* (1571). I turn to it, in conclusion, because of the crucial position held by St Teresa in the history of Western mysticism at the moment when contemplative experience looked, self-reflexively, at its own implicit structure while seeking conformity, still, to ecclesial tradition.[11] All significant modern Catholic debate, writes a scholar of the subject,[12] takes its starting point from the decisiveness of St Teresa's examination of the differences between ordinary and extraordinary prayer, acquired and infused contemplation: differences, that is, which distinguish mysticism as a special condition of Christian life.

St Teresa, we should note first, wrote under obedience, and keeps reminding us that she would not have undertaken the task on her own initiative: 'I am so stupid in these matters' (p. 56). She proceeds willingly, however, on recalling that her instruction may help a reader to pray more effectively: 'If it only enables a single person to praise Him once, I think it is a good thing that all this should be said' (p. 68).

Clearly, Teresa's superiors knew she had valuable teachings to convey to her 'daughters', and we can be thankful that their constraint led to the composition of a book we would not otherwise have. For her part, Teresa is deferential to authority, and, as commentators point out, she is careful not only to proclaim her ignorance of theology, but to describe her unusual experiences with circumspection, and to avoid suggesting that she may be subversive or heterodox. Despite her pains, the Inquisition did, at first, condemn her *Life*, and part of Teresa's unwillingness to take up her pen a second time was doubtless because she would be exposed again to inquisitorial scrutiny.

We would be wrong, however, to regard Teresa as weakly submissive. Her apprehension is rooted in her knowledge that men in authority are too often ignorant and inexperienced, and therefore sometimes dangerous. Teresa did not have the freedom of, say, an Erasmus[13] to criticise ecclesiastical abuses, and her circumstances and commitment ruled out sympathy for the Northern Reformers. Still, by experience Teresa knew that rules, regulations and dogmatic preconceptions could easily interfere with spiritual progress, and, consequently, in the *Interior Castle* there is a good deal critical of unsatisfactory spiritual directors. 'I am very ready to give credence to those who have great learning' (p. 100), Teresa writes, because God uses such men to give light to his church. But she has also had 'experience of timid, half-learned men whose shortcomings have cost me very dear'. Elsewhere she criticises a confessor who rushes to exaggerated conclusions in the teeth of commonsense: 'He thinks that people to whom God grants these [spiritual] favours must be angels; and, as this is impossible while they are in the body, he attributes the whole thing to melancholy or to the devil' (p. 130). Certain directors seem even to aid the devil in tormenting souls (p. 130), and, at one point, Teresa describes bad instruction given by a confessor, and counters it: 'My own advice is that, if you are given such counsel, you should not accept it . . .' (p. 190).

Readers of *The Interior Castle,* in short, can scarcely doubt Teresa's independence, and there is even a sense that the learned authorities who instructed her to write for her spiritual daughters were really interested in receiving some edification themselves, which Teresa took the opportunity to provide. Of course, her primary audience remains 'the nuns of these convents of Our Lady of Carmel', as we are reminded throughout by direct address: ('You will desire, then, my daughters' [p. 83]; 'Oh Sisters!' [p. 96]; 'I tell you, daughters' [p. 120]).

Finally, we may conjecture, Teresa herself learned something. Direct communication ('I will tell you what I have found out' [p. 83]), can quickly pass into exasperation and chagrin ('Oh, Jesus! How I wish I could make myself clear about this' [p. 74]). Instruction delivered from 'I' to 'you' often becomes exploratory, an exchange in which 'we' share ('I will tell you about some of them so that we may learn to understand . . . ." [p. 63]). The act of writing itself becomes a means of enlightenment for the author, and sentences throughout suggest that Teresa was discovering this with some pleasure: 'I do not think I have ever explained this before as clearly as here' (p. 86); 'Really, sisters, the mere writing of this makes me astounded . . . ." (p. 158).

The sisters thus find practical instruction, the authorities wisdom, and the author understanding: we need to help others in whatever way we can; we need to be instructed; we need to clarify our experience to ourselves. Teresa's teaching involves the constant interaction of all three elements, suggesting that, in various combinations, they open up different possibilities, different directions, for different readers. Teresa well knew that the 'ways' in which God leads souls are manifold, so that it is impossible to be completely clear on the subject. There is 'no infallible rule' (p. 73), and 'no reason why we should expect everyone else to travel by our own road' (p. 69). The castle which, as the title indicates, Teresa takes for her key metaphor, has many mansions. One Lord dwells at the centre, but the rooms arranged in concentric circles around his chamber are innumerable and various: 'there are so many of them that nobody can possibly understand them all' (pp. 29–30). Teresa repeatedly forces this insight upon her readers, partly out of humility, though humility recognises also how presumptuous it is to take any path completely 'untrodden' (p. 231).

In context of such qualifications presented through the full display of her argument, Teresa undertakes also to describe and classify certain typical interior experiences. She distinguishes, for instance, between imagination and understanding, the prayer of recollection and the prayer of quiet, imaginary and intellectual visions, various kinds of rapture, soul and spirit. In the seven-fold division of the castle into rooms or 'Mansions', she indicates a progress from asceticism through recollection, quiet, inter-mittent union, to spiritual marriage, which is a foretaste of heaven (p. 212). There is order here, though Teresa resists pre-scription, and we are left with a sense that she herself is discovering the 'way' as she proceeds along it. Fifteen years ago, she reminds us (referring to her *Life*), she had described the prayer of quiet differently (p. 83). Things are now more clear, even though 'Both then and now, of course, I may be mistaken in all this' (p. 83).

Although she talks, therefore, of a 'way' to God, and describes some of its phases, Teresa does not confuse her map with reality, and her definitions merge easily with metaphors and similitudes. Imagination, she claims, is in closest conformity with our nature (p. 185), and mediates between corporeal and intellectual. It is, however, ambiguous, and is one of the Devil's most useful weapons (p. 116). But Teresa does not hesitate to deploy the devil's weapons against him, and her writing is rich in imagina-tive representations of spiritual truths. The mind is a crystal covered with cloth (p. 36), a palm which contains a kernel under layers of leaves (p. 37), a bird with a broken wing (p. 59), and a clacking mill (p. 79). We are asked to consider the flight of bees (p. 37), the action of a file (p. 42), of a hedgehog and a tortoise (p. 87), of fountains and conduits (pp. 80ff.), the metamorphosis of silkworms to butterflies (pp. 104ff.), the flight of doves (pp. 11ff.), the behaviour of straw attracted by amber (p. 158). But we are warned too about weak and sickly imaginations (p. 94), and constantly we are reminded of the limits of imaginative representation: 'I only put it in that way so that you may understand it' (p. 82). Teresa insists, rather, on the delicacy (p. 82) of spiritual states, especially the sort she calls 'intellectual vision'. We may talk about 'sight' in this context, she says, but it is not literal sight (p. 126); about matrimony, but not literally (p. 118); about locution, but not, literally, as audible speech (p. 86). 'It may happen', we are told, 'that, while the soul is not in the least expecting Him to be about to grant it this favour, which it has never thought it can possibly deserve, it is conscious that Jesus Christ Our Lord is near to it, though it cannot see Him either with the eyes of the body or with those of the soul. This (I do not know why) is called an intellectual vision' (p. 179). Teresa describes the experience of an anonymous 'she' (who we must suppose is herself): 'She was conscious that He was walking at her right hand, but this consciousness arose, not from those senses which tell us that another person is near us, but in another and a subtler way which is indescribable' (p. 180).

There is a great deal about intellectual vision in the *Interior Castle*, and Teresa is constantly bothered by the failure of language and imagination to convey her meaning. She is aware, too, that it can be embarrassing and futile to have to write a book in such circumstances. The sceptical reader, after all (whether a sixteenth-century Dominican or present-day sceptic), is likely to wonder about the woman's soundness of mind. But Teresa provides reassurance: if 'imagination' is the most characteristic mode of human discourse, and if it fails to communicate purely 'intellectual' intuitions, these intuitions must validate themselves in the 'corporeal' world. Thus, to offset her most ineffable claims, Teresa is imaginative enough to be concertedly practical. We must look to concrete results for indications that claims made in the name of higher vision are to be taken seriously. The real test is whether love of our neighbour is increased (pp. 114ff.), for 'what the Lord desires is works' (p. 116). The surest, publicly evident, mark of genuine vision is tranquillity, based on certainty that from a life centred in Christ proceed good deeds. Teresa's insistence on this point imparts to her book a quality of practical sturdiness, despite its often sublime divagations. More food and sleep and less penance (p. 93) will cure some so-called 'visions'; whatever ruins your health cannot be good (p. 42), though overcautious hypochondria can also be debilitating (p. 65); psychologically sick persons sometimes need to be humoured to prevent their condition from worsening (p. 139); we should not always seek advice from others of the same temperament as ourselves, for that is insufficiently corrective (p. 68); people are not angels, and we should not be impatient of their imperfections (p. 130).

Nonetheless, Teresa assures us, we must strive to make progress, for not to advance once we have set out on the course of spiritual life is dangerous (p. 122). Indeed the road – the many roads – are all dangerous, and there runs throughout the *Interior Castle* a profound wisdom of insecurity. The story of Judas, we are told, should convince us that safety is never guaranteed (p. 121), and there is no escape from the trials of this life, or from the cross. The lesson is repeated at every stage, with respect to every mansion. Even in the spiritual marriage, where we find rest, we do not find security because we must return to the world (p. 225), working out, through the complex paths of a shared destiny, a way which remains unique to each of us.

St Teresa's description of the life of prayer and of her own spiritual development comprises all of these teachings and attitudes, synthesised through her personal vision. The way, thus presented, confirms our shared implication with culture, with history and with circumstance. The elements in the process involve the rigour of reasoned enquiry no less than the spontaneity of personal insight and the immediacy of dialogue. Classification, though clear, is flexible, and a variety of imaginative insights and metaphors gives it life and ensures suppleness. Discussion of the ineffable is grounded in good sense, validated in a hard-headed assessment of practical results. In no 'method' describable by language, we are told, lies security; and Teresa's prose,[14] impatient with itself, winningly artless, digressive, whimsical and precise by turns, constantly reminds us that the end of such writing is not the work itself, but the service it might provide to those who know the difference between words and works. Yet in those effects which Teresa describes as 'delicate' and 'subtle', and which she explicates with all the range of intelligence, intuition and imagination at her disposal, we continue to detect an excellence to which the word 'poetry' applies. The language, we might say, achieves distinction analogous to the quality of life the author prescribes, likewise combining radiance, harmony and wholeness. Perhaps acknowledgement of such achievement, both in art and in life, encouraged Simone de Beauvoir to write that 'there is hardly a woman other than St Teresa who in total abandonment has lived out the situation of humanity'.[15] An unlikely compliment, considering Mme de Beauvoir's atheism; but then not all proceed by the same paths, and, as Teresa says, we are likely to be amazed at how different God's judgement of our fellow humans will be, in the end, 'from the ideas we have formed on earth' (p. 184).

TEXTS WITHOUT COMMENT

6 THE WAY

1. This is perfect love. But it may not incongruously be asked whether this standing in love, once had, may at any time be lost. Truly whiles man can sin he can lose charity; but not to be able to sin belongs not to the state of this way but of the country above: wherefore ilk man, howsoever holy he be in this life, yet he can sin and mortally; for the dregs of sin are fully slakened in no pilgrim of this life after common law.

Richard Rolle (c. 1300–49),
The Fire of Love, Ch. XIX

2. Now in this manner, even as one star differeth from another in brightness, so one cell differeth from another in conversation, that is to say conversation of those beginning, of those advancing, and of those that are perfect. The state of beginners may be called animal; of those advancing, rational; of the perfect, spiritual.

William of St Thierry (1085–1148),
Golden Epistle, 5, 12

3. He that dares not say an ill-natured word, or do an unreasonable thing, because he considers God as everywhere present, performs a better devotion, than he that dares not miss the church. To live in the world as a stranger and a pilgrim, using all its enjoyments as if we used them not, making all our actions so many steps towards a better life, is

offering a better sacrifice to God, than any forms of holy and
heavenly prayers.

William Law (1686–1761),
A Serious Call, Ch. x

4. Suppose a man embarks upon a certain course, starts this
work or gives up that, and then some accident befalls, he
breaks his arm or leg perhaps, loses an eye or falls ill. If he
keeps on saying to himself, hadst thou pursued a different
course or done otherwise this would never have had
occurred, he will remain disconsolate and is bound to suffer.
But if he argues with himself, hadst thou taken any other
step, done or forborne to do some thing, a much worse fate
might have been thine, he will soon take heart and feel more
cheerful.

Meister Eckhart (1260–1327),
The Book of Benedictus, i, 2

5. For it is permitted to no man long to remain in the same
state, but always the servant of God must needs advance, or
else fall away; either he striveth upwards or he is driven
downwards.

William of St Thierry (1085–1148)
Golden Epistle, 4, 11

6. For even so a man that taketh a journey any whither, if he
holdeth to no one sure road, shall quickly come thither
whither he goeth and make and end of his journey and of his
toil. But if he essay many roads, he wandereth and maketh
never an end of his toil, because of such wandering there is
no end.

William of St Thierry (1085–1148),
Golden Epistle, 9, 26

7. Farther I understand, that from their thus feeling themselves
on one part prized, loved, and favoured of God, and on the
other part despised, persecuted, and hated of the world, it
redounds, that they following where the holy spirit leads
them, running after Faith, Hope, and Charity, esteem
themselves Pilgrims in this present life, esteeming themselves Cittizens of eternall life.

Juan de Valdes (1490–1541),
Considerations, xcvi

8. He who insists on being left to himself, without a director to
guide him, is like an unowned tree by the wayside; however

fruitful it may be, the travellers pick its fruit, and none of it ripens.

John of the Cross (1542–91),
Spiritual Maxims, 178

9. It is a miserable thing to see how this Employment of directing soules (which above all other is most difficult and exceedeth even the ability of an Angell' yet) out of an ambitious humour is invaded by persons wholly unfitted for it, and that without any vocation from God voluntarily undertake it. So that no mervaile it is if so little good come from such Intruders. Not one of a thousand (saith Avila) is capable of so sublime a taske. Nay saith the holy Bishop of Geneva, not one of ten thousand. And most certeine it is, that those who so freely offer themselves to so Divine an employment, doe thereby shew themselves to want the most necessary qualifications, to wit, Humility and a true knowledge of its difficulty, and therfore their directions are most to be suspected.

Augustine Baker (1575–1641),
Sancta Sophia, Treatise I, 74

10. If a soule that is fearfull and scrupulous be to chuse a Directour, she ought to avoyd one of the like temper, for passion which blinds the seeker, will also blind the Directour, and so the Blind will leade the blind.

Augustine Baker (1575–1641),
Sancta Sophia, Treatise I, 75

11. As confessors cannot see these effects, which perhaps the person to whom God has shown the vision is unable to explain, they are afraid of deception, as indeed they have good reason to be. Therefore caution is necessary and time should be allowed to see what results follow. Day by day, the progress of the soul in humility and in the virtues should be watched: if the devil is concerned in the matter, he will soon show signs of himself and will be detected in a thousand lies. If the confessor is experienced and has received such favours himself, he will not take long in discovering the truth. In fact, he will know immediately, on being told of the vision, whether it is divine or comes from the imagination or the demon: more especially if he has received the gift of discerning spirits – then, if he is learned, he will understand the matter at once even though he has not personally

experienced the like.

Teresa of Avila (1515–82),
Interior Castle, Sixth Mansion, IX, 9

12. Here Junius said to his Master; This is hard to understand. Doth it not enter into Heaven or Hell, as a Man entereth into an House; or as one goeth through an Hole or Casement, into an unknown Place; so goeth it not into another World?

The Master spake and said; No. There is verily no such Kind of entering in; forasmuch as Heaven and Hell are every where, being universally co-extended.

How is that possible? said the Scholar. What, can Heaven and Hell be here present, where we are now sitting? And if one of them might, can you make me believe that ever both should be here together?

Then spoke the Master in this Manner: I have said that Heaven is every where present; and it is true. For God is in Heaven; and God is every where. I have said also, that Hell must be in like Manner every where; and that is also true. For the wicked One, who is the Devil, is in Hell; and the whole World, as the Apostle hath taught us, lyeth in the wicked One, or the evil One; which is as much as to say, not only that the Devil is in the World, but also that the World is in the Devil; and if in the Devil, then in Hell too, because he is there. So Hell therefore is every where, as well as Heaven; which is the Thing that was to be proved.

The Scholar startled hereat, said, Pray make me to understand this.

To whom the Master: Understand then what Heaven is: It is but the turning in of the Will into the Love of God. Wheresoever thou findest God manifesting himself in Love, there thou findest Heaven, without travelling for it so much as one Foot. And by this understand also what hell is, and where it is. I say unto thee, it is but the turning in of the Will into the Wrath of God.

Jacob Boehme (1575–1624),
The Way to Christ, IV

13. Now understand this well: that measureless Splendour of God, which together with the incomprehensible brightness, is the cause of all gifts and of all virtues – that same Uncomprehended Light transfigures the fruitive tendency of our spirit and penetrates it in a way that is wayless; that is, through the Uncomprehended Light. And in this light the

spirit immerses itself in fruitive rest; for this rest is wayless and fathomless, and one can know of it in no other way than through itself – that is, through rest. For, could we know and comprehend it, it would fall into mode and measure; then it could not satisfy us, but rest would become an eternal restlessness. And for this reason, the simple, loving and immersed tendency of our spirit works within us a fruitive love; and this fruitive love is abysmal. And the abyss of God calls to the abyss; that is, of all those who are united with the Spirit of God in fruitive love. This inward call is an inundation of the essential brightness, and this essential brightness, enfolding us in an abysmal love, causes us to be lost to ourselves, and to flow forth from ourselves into the wild darkness of the Godhead.

John of Ruysbroeck (1293–1381),
Adornment of the Spiritual Marriage, Ch. LXIV

14. The paths must also be made straight from within; we must seek them diligently; our spirits in God and God in us; for the paths are dark and unknown. Many men go astray, running after external works and discipline.

John Tauler (c. 1300–61), Sermon,
'On the Feast of the Nativity of St
John the Baptist'

15. Let us then avoid custom as we would a dangerous headland, or the threatening Charybdis, or the mythic sirens. It chokes man, turns him away from truth, leads him away from life: custom is a snare, a gulf, a pit, a mischievous winnowing fan.

Clement of Alexandria (c. 160–220),
Exhortation to the Heathen, XII

16. The man said, 'Tell me, Beloved, what is the reason that the men on this ninth rock shine inwardly like bright angels?' The answer came: 'God has filled these men with luminous grace so that it must shine forth from them; but they neither know it nor wish to know'. The man said: 'Beloved, are there many of these men, for I think them to be the righteous men?' The answer came: 'I will tell you. As few as they are, for their sake God permits Christendom to continue. You see, if these men were gone, God would immediately let Christendom perish'.

Rulman Merswin (c. 1310–82),
Book of the Nine Rocks

17. The man said: 'O Beloved, I am sure that there are still men who would ascend the true road if they but knew of it'. The answer came: 'No one is guiltless, whoever knows the best way will take it. Whoever has reached the age of reason, even though he lie bound in sin under the mist, will know that God is merciful, and if he strive with all his might and courage, he will know that God will have pity on his struggles, will offer him his hand and lead him out from the mist if only he will follow him with his whole heart'.

Rulman Merswin (c. 1310–82),
Book of the Nine Rocks

18. But from the lowest to the highest a soul may not suddenly start, no more than a man that will climb upon a ladder high and setteth his foot upon the lowest rung may at the next fly up to the highest; but it behoveth him to go by process one after another till he may come to the topmost. Right so is it ghostly; no man is made suddenly sovereign in grace, but through long exercise and sly working a soul may come thereto, namely when He helpeth and teacheth a wretched soul in whom all grace lieth. For without special help and inwardly teaching of Him may no soul come thereto.

Walter Hilton (–1396),
Scale of Perfection, II, 17

19. The same spirit needs no ladder nor requires to be supported in the subtility of his ascent by the shadow of any material images, there where he shall see face to face and not in a glass darkly. Truly I lie if the same is not asserted of themselves, by those who share this experience, for they say: 'But we all, with open face beholding as in a glass the glory of the Lord, are changed into the same image from glory to glory, even as by the spirit of the Lord'.

Richard of St Victor (–c. 1173),
De Exterminatione Mali, III, 18

20. Now severall Mysticke Authours according to the severall Notions that they had both of the End of a Spirituall Life, and Meanes conducing thereto, have by severall termes made the Division of its Degrees. The most ancient Division is into three states, 1. Of Beginners. 2. Of Proficients. 3. Of such as are Perfect. Yet withall they doe not signify by what distinctive Markes each of these States are separated from the others. But generally in latter times the whole course of a

Spirituall Life is divided. 1. Into the Purgative way: in which all sinfull Defects are purged out of the Soule. 2. The Illuminative way, by which Divine Vertues and Graces are introduced. 3. The Unitive way, by which a Soule attaines unto the End of all other Exercises, to wit, on Union with God in Spirit by perfect Charity.

Augustine Baker (1575–1641),
Sancta Sophia, Treatise III, 83–4

21. Thus there are three stages: first, the purification; secondly, the enlightening; thirdly, the union. The purification concerneth those who are beginning or repenting, and is brought to pass in a threefold wise; by contrition and sorrow for sin, by full confession, by hearty amendment. The enlightening belongeth to such as are growing, and also taketh place in three ways: to wit, by the eschewal of sin, by the practice of virtue and good works, and by the willing endurance of all manner of temptation and trials. The union belongeth to such as are perfect, and also is brought to pass in three ways: to wit, by pureness and singleness of heart, by love, and by the contemplation of God, the Creator of all things.

Theologia Germanica (c. 1350), Ch. XIV

22. For almighty God created three kinds of spirits having life. One altogether spiritual without body: another with a body, but yet which dieth not with the body: the third that which is both joined with the body, and also together with the body doth die. The spirits that have no bodies be the Angels: they that have bodies but die not with them, be the souls of men: those that have bodies and die together with them, be the souls of cattle and brute beasts. Man, therefore, as he is created in the middle state, inferior to Angels and superior to beasts, so doth he participate of both: having immortality of soul with the Angels, and mortality of body with beasts, until the day of doom.

Gregory the Great (540–604),
The Dialogues, Bk. IV Ch. 3

CHAPTER SEVEN
Conclusion

Mysticism, in the tradition with which this book deals, can be described as an experimental knowledge of God in which ordinary perception and discursive thought are transcended by a sense of union. The mystic is solitary, but not isolated, because the meaning of his experience joins him to a human community. Being alive in the body, self-conscious through a particular language and type of education, he is predisposed to certain kinds of experience and modes of understanding. And because it is humanly impossible to separate the meaning of experience from its expression, the cycle of vision and interpretation places mysticism within the process of culture.

Vision of God is of course ineffable, but we can judge, partially, a person's insight by attending to results. In some such manner, mystics are empiricists, asking us to concede that the fruits of their actions justify our investigation of their claims. Poised on the boundaries of human discourse, they maintain a dialogue between a culture's articulate framework and the spirit which gives it life, drawing upon and challenging the deepest resources of faith without which, in the end, there is no understanding. In their lives we are to detect a quality of wholeness and beauty, a poetry of conduct which, they maintain, is the fruit of a God-centred existence. To discount their vision of God would be to impugn, in some degree, the integrity of their behaviour in other respects.

Writing takes its place among the works of men, including mystics, and it has been a chief concern of this book. Literature of mysticism, however, consistently draws attention to the insufficiency of words, and insists on the differences between language and deeds: even while deploying the deed of language, mystics remind us of its limited efficacy. But the Negative Way does not exist in complete separation from the Affirmative, as literature of mysticism acknowledges by undertaking in the first place to describe, through language, the way of silence.

Not all writing, of course, even on the highest forms of experience, realises the highest virtue of literature, and the spiritual handbooks often give us wholesome, but dull, advice. Poetry requires the revelation, also, of some quality of life in the form of words, a certain genius of character which brings illumination, which is filled with intellectual discernment and subtlety of feeling – the music of thought, as Rolle says, distinctive for its style, its sense of depth, as well as for its good sense. In this respect, the language of poetry is the most satisfactory natural analogue for the mystical life which, we might say, expresses through action the poetry of religion.

Although the roots of literature and mysticism are thus intertwined, poets bear witness first to the process of natural significance, and their aim is to produce works of art. Mystics call attention rather to the supernatural in which signs are transformed in the intuitive bliss of immediate and glorious intelligibility, and their aim is union with God. Because it is misleading, even futile, to seek an understanding of mysticism without belief, the perennial intuitions of the mystics are best apprehended through an appreciation of whatever particular circumstances enable one to speak most fully on the question. One's tradition is, in this sense, one's best language and principal safeguard against the simplistic and illusory. But mystics, like poets, are not tradition-bound: they are surprising, and remain open to surprises, though these are of a sort which fulfil unformed desires and expectations, rather than induce disorientation and uncertainty. Contradictions among religious faiths, it follows, are likely to be overcome less by an anxious abandonment of one's position than by practice of charity and the gradual appropriation of other points of view, a process in which dogmas and symbols can take on an enhanced life, discovering, as it were, their own deepest possibilities. In such an exchange the kinds of differences which cause division (rather than variety) should dwindle by neglect. To assist such progress, we must be willing at least to stand upon the boundaries of our tradition according to our capacities, reaching to all that our tradition seems to reject: a position, that is, analogous to the poet's, using the common language to test common ideas in his singular manner.

Consequently, these essays are about Western tradition and reflect a certain understanding of some of its elements. The argument suggests that imagination, rooted in attention, is a self-authenticating activity bringing to light the natural miracle of self-consciousness. In his theory of 'spiritual vision', St Augustine grasped at imagination's dual yet synthesising activity through the doctrine of Incarnation. In the subsequent history of Western literature, 'spiritual vision' was to become increasingly preoccupied with itself as an engenderer of images: a lamp of inspiration, not the mirror of God's design. In the course of such a development, culminating in the Romantic movement, imagination knew itself distinct from conceptual thought pertaining to man's supernatural end. Consequently, poets and theologians felt themselves responsible for discrete, rather than necessarily co-implicated realms of discourse. Poetry could challenge, even rebuke, the God of theologians as well as (even better than) it could vindicate him.

Entranced, however, by its power as magus and creator, the Romantically self-preoccupied ego is tempted to perilous autonomy, and mystics consistently warn against such a danger. Yet ego remains a vehicle of culture and morality, and the first step to wisdom is not its annihilation, but mortification. We are to accept ego and the death of ego as Christ accepted the cross, so that Christ can live in us, the truest expression of our selves. But adjusting the dynamics of self and ego calls for the tact of a poet, as Spenser saw, and poetry's analogue to mortification is in that form of self-expression which dispenses with, and so mortifies, the merely individualistic. Indeed, in a special sense, literature of mysticism in the Latin West finds its subject in the cross. Representing the incompleteness of symbols, the cross brings home the failure of imagination to depict mystery, and the best devotional poetry is about problems of faith, which the cross traditionally signifies and which poetry can better express than solve. But because the poet knows psyche's subterfuges and complexities, he can, with special authority, warn against the violence of simplistic asceticism and naive idealism. Poetry uniquely can tell how the crucifixion of God recurs when, from ego's terror and anxiety issues an infliction of suffering on one's self, or others.

Crucifixion, Incarnation, Trinity and the Oneness of God: none of these can be understood in isolation from the others, and the mystical theologian sustains their interaction through a vision enlivening dogma's arbitrariness, galvanising its incompleteness to express a certain relationship to reality which the church in its wisdom has refrained from defining, but from which it takes its life, and which we call 'mysticism'. The vision is renewed perennially in a variety of tongues and cultures and personalities, and is not separate from the history from which it emerges but resolutely refuses to idolise. It draws us in the direction of an enhanced life within a physical world blessed with significance such as poets discover, where the instruments of science should turn to the relief of suffering by the direction of the Spirit through whose light the instruments themselves have come into our hands. The ways and means of Spirit perennially remain various, alive in the quality of a deed, as the poet's particular voice, though showing forth universals, comes alive in a style of discourse. And by such ways and means we are urged to acknowledge that even propositions as deeply challenging to common sense as those of the mystics may call upon and deserve our open-minded attention.

Notes

CHAPTER 1: MYSTICISM, FAITH AND CULTURE

1. On solitude and isolation, see Thomas Merton, *New Seeds of Contemplation* (New York: New Directions, 1972), pp. 52 ff.
2. 'Expression' indicates not only writing, but all the forms of human expression, including one's actions and the quality of one's life. Most standard works deal with the term 'mysticism': see further, Louis Bouyer, 'Mysticism: An Essay on the History of a Word', in *Mystery and Mysticism: A Symposium*, A. Plé (ed.) (New York: Philosophical Library, 1956), pp. 119–37.
3. For analysis of the 'tacit component' from which we attend to things, see especially the works of Michael Polanyi, for example, *The Tacit Dimension* (New York: Doubleday, 1966); *Personal Knowledge: Towards a Post-Critical Philosophy* (New York: Harper Torchbooks, 1964); with Harry Prosch, *Meaning* (Chicago: University of Chicago Press, 1975). On the 'double anonymity' mentioned above, see Maurice Merleau-Ponty, *Phenomenology of Perception*, trans. Colin Smith (London: Routledge and Kegan Paul, 1962), pp. 448, *et passim*. For an interesting synthesis of Polanyi and Merleau-Ponty, see Marjorie Grene, *The Knower and the Known* (Berkeley: University of California Press, 1974). Professor Grene's book is not concerned with mysticism, but her synthesis has much to offer to students of the subject.
4. Spiritual Canticle, XXXV, 3, trans. E. Allison Peers, *The Complete Works of Saint John of the Cross*, 3 vols. (Hertfordshire: Anthony Clarke, 1974. First published, 1935), II, 154.
5. *Objective Knowledge. An Evolutionary Approach* (Oxford: Clarendon Press, 1972), p. 72.
6. AE (George William Russell), *The Candle of Vision. The Autobiography of a Mystic* (Illinois: Theosophical Publishing House, 1974), p. 20.
7. St Teresa of Avila, *Interior Castle*, trans. E. Allison Peers (New York: Image Books, 1961), p. 116.
8. 'The "Logic of God"', in *The Existence of God*, ed. John Hick (London: Collier-Macmillan, 1964), pp. 275–98. W. T. Stace, *Mysticism and Philosophy* (London: Macmillan, 1960), pp. 134 ff., deals with the problem of objectivity in mystical experience. See further, J. Gilbert, 'Mystical Experience and Public Testability', *Sophia* (1970), vol. 9, pp. 13–20; William James, *The Varieties of Religious Experience. A Study in Human Nature* (London: Collier, 1960. First published, 1901–2), pp. 408, 490.
9. W. R. Inge, *Mysticism in Religion* (London: Hutchinson's University Library, 1947), p. 148, argues that, philosophically, mysticism rests on

discovering unity in duality. Not all discussions assume that mysticism has to do with God. See, for instance, Frits Staal, *Exploring Mysticism. A Methodological Essay* (Berkeley: University of California Press, 1975), p. 190; W. T. Stace, *The Teachings of the Mystics* (New York: New American Library, 1960), p. 23; *Mysticism and Philosophy*, pp. 178, 341, *et passim*.

10. A. Poulain, S.J., *The Graces of Interior Prayer*, trans. Leonora L. Yorke Smith (London: Routledge and Kegan Paul, 1950), xii, note 2; xiii, 4, 1; lxxxix, 28; 353, 13; 539; 579, 46. On rapprochment between mysticism and science, see Stanley R. Dean (ed.), *Psychiatry and Mysticism* (Chicago: Nelson Hall, 1975); Alister Hardy, *The Spiritual Nature of Man* (Oxford: Clarendon Press, 1979); Charles T. Tart (ed.), *Transpersonal Psychologies* (London: Routledge and Kegan Paul, 1975).

11. This kind of philosophical theory, suggesting that wherever there are procedures there are things assumed known without procedures, is discussed with respect to mystical experience by Renford Bambrough, 'Intuition and the Inexpressible', in *Mysticism and Philosophical Analysis*, Steven T. Katz (ed.) (London: Sheldon Press, 1978), pp. 200 ff. With respect to theology, see R. Garrigou-Legrange, *Christian Perfection and Contemplation*, trans. Sister M. Timothea Doyle (London and St. Louis: B. Herder Book Co., 1937), which holds that mysticism is the plenitude of the life of faith.

12. Aldous Huxley, *The Perennial Philosophy* (New York: Harper, 1970. First published, 1944), p. 132: 'Thus mystics make theology, and theology makes mystics'.

13. R. C. Zaehner, *Mysticism Sacred and Profane. An Inquiry into some Varieties of Praeternatural Experience* (London: Oxford University Press, 1961. First published, 1957), p. 8.

14. See Charles Darwin, *The Autobiography of Charles Darwin*, Nora Barlow (ed.) (London: Collins, 1958), pp. 138, 115.

15. See Herbert Thurston, *Surprising Mystics*, J. H. Crelan (ed.) (London: Burns and Oates, 1955).

16. See Patrick Grant, *Six Modern Authors and Problems of Belief* (London: Macmillan, 1979), Ch. 2, 'Belief in Mysticism: Aldous Huxley, from Grey Eminence to Island', pp. 17–39.

17. Gai Eaton, *The Richest Vein. Eastern Tradition and Modern Thought* (London: Faber and Faber, 1949), Ch. 8, 'Monk at Large: Aldous Huxley', pp. 166–82, assesses Huxley's understanding of 'perennial philosophy', and objects that 'he has undertaken a labour of selection and rejection which no man on earth is entitled to undertake' (p. 182).

18. A key term in Rudolf Otto's *The Idea of the Holy*, trans. J. W. Harvey (Aberdeen: H. W. Turner, 1974). See further, A. C. Bouquet, *Comparative Religion* (Harmondsworth: Penguin Books, 1969. First published, 1941), pp. 20–8; Eric J. Sharpe, 'The Comparative Study of Religion in Historical Perspective', in *Man's Religious Quest. A Reader*, Whitfield Foy (ed.) (London: Croom Helm, in association with the Open University Press, 1978), pp. 7–21. Sharpe points out that Darwin's *Origin of Species* was a turning point, after which we find a new class of scholar, such as Max Müller, E. B. Tylor, J. G. Frazer, R. R. Marett, and others.

19. Jacob Needleman (ed.), *The Sword of Gnosis* (Baltimore: Penguin Books,

1974), p. 9. This volume contains a representative sample of essays, and has a good bibliography.

20. This summary of Guénon's main arguments can be followed up in *The Crisis of the Modern World*, trans. Marco Pallis and Richard Nicholson (London: Luzac, 1975. First published, 1942), and *The Reign of Quantity and the Signs of the Times* (London: Luzac, 1953).

21. See *Mysticism Sacred and Profane*, pp. 30 ff.

22. *Crisis of the Modern World*, pp. 10, 110.

23. See Ninian Smart, 'Understanding Religious Experience', in *Mysticism and Philosophical Analysis*, Katz (ed.), p. 13. See also James R. Horne, *Beyond Mysticism* (Toronto: Canadian Corporation for Studies in Religion, 1978), pp. 31 ff, and Frits Staal, *Exploring Mysticism*, pp. 67–9.

24. Paul Tillich's insistence on ultimate values implied by the ambiguity of ordinary knowledge is helpful as a reassurance about the humanising nature of mysticism. See, for instance, *Systematic Theology* (Chicago: University of Chicago Press, 1951–63), Vol. III, pp. 241 ff., *et passim*.

25. On this 'ordinary' aspect of mysticism, see James R. Horne, *Beyond Mysticism*, p. 69: 'Mysticism resembles other reasonable problem-solving procedures'. See also David Knowles, *The English Mystical Tradition* (London: Burns and Oates, 1961), p. 18: united to God, a person has 'more truly than before, a fully developed personality'.

26. See Jacques Maritain, *Creative Intuition in Art and Poetry* (New Jersey: Princeton University Press, 1953; paperback edition, 1977), pp. 234 ff., for a description of this distinction. Also, Jacques and Raissa Maritain, *The Situation of Poetry* (New York: Philosophical Library, 1955).

27. Thomas Merton, *Contemplation in a World of Action* (New York: Image Books, 1973) pp. 251 ff., makes clear that the hermit 'owes his solitude' (p. 256) to the community. For an analysis, along Kantian lines, of how mysticism grasps at 'frontiers', see Donald M. MacKinnon, 'Some Epistemological Reflections on Mystical Experience', in *Mysticism and Philosophical Analysis*, Katz (ed.), p. 139. J. H. W. Whiteman, *The Mystical Life* (London: Faber and Faber, 1961), p. 165, asks us not to become confounded by 'distracting questions and difficulties', but 'to absorb instead the flavour and illumination of the inner worlds'.

28. 'Understanding Religious Experience', p. 20.

29. *Sacramentum Mundi*, Karl Rahner (ed.) (New York: Herder, 1968–70), art. 'Mysticism', p. 138.

30. See *Discernment of Spirits*, Jacques Guillet *et al.* (eds.), trans. Sister Innocentia Richards (Minnesota: Liturgical Press, 1970).

31. See Jean de Menasce, 'The Experience of the Spirit in Christian Mysticism', in *The Mystic Vision. Papers from the Eranos Yearbooks*, trans. Ralph Manheim (New Jersey: Princeton University Press, 1968), pp. 328 ff.

32. The *Incendium Amoris* of Richard Rolle of Hampole, Margaret Deanesly (ed.) (Manchester: Manchester University Press, 1915), is the standard Latin text. The following quotations are taken from *The Fire of Love*, trans. Clifton Wolters (Harmondsworth: Penguin Books, 1972). Page numbers are cited in the text.

33. See R. W. Chambers, *On the Continuity of English Prose from Alfred to More*

and his School, E. V. Hitchcock and R. W. Chambers (eds.), Early English Text Society, Old Series, 191a (London: Oxford University Press, 1932), p. ci: examination of English wills and documents bearing on the ownership of books 'seems to show a dozen owners of manuscripts of Rolle for one or two of the Canterbury Tales'; E. J. Arnould, 'Richard Rolle of Hampole', in *Pre-Reformation English Spirituality*, James Walsh (ed.) (New York: Fordham University Press, 1965), p. 138; *Incendium Amoris*, Deanesly (ed.), 'Introduction. (1) Description of Manuscripts', pp. 1 ff.

34. Rosemary Woolf, *The English Religious Lyric in the Middle Ages* (Oxford: Clarendon Press, 1968), p. 159: 'there can be no doubt that it was the work of Rolle and the outstanding authority of his name that restored the prestige of English as a medium for contemplative writing'.

35. Wolters, *The Fire of Love*, pp. 11 ff., gives a concise biographical account.

36. The Latin is 'quasi cum quadam pneuma canens'. The word 'qualitas' is not used.

37. Wallace Stevens, 'Peter Quince at the Clavier'; Jacques Maritain, *Creative Intuition*, p. 302.

38. See also, pp. 114, 120, 131, 144, 179.

39. See Knowles, *The English Mystical Tradition*, p. 52; Arnould, 'Richard Rolle', p. 139; Geraldine E. Hodgson, *The Sanity of Mysticism. A Study of Richard Rolle* (London: Faith Press, 1926), pp. 102 ff.

40. Mary Felicitas Madigan, The 'Passio Domini' Theme in the Works of Richard Rolle: His Personal Contribution in its Religious, Cultural, and Literary Context (Salzburg: Institut für Englisch Sprache und Literatur, 1978), analyses Rolle's style in some detail, with reference to rhetorical tradition. Chambers, *On the Continuity of English Prose*, p. cii, points out that Rolle was still in touch with older stages of the language. See also, Richard H. Osberg, 'The Alliterative Theory and Thirteenth Century Devotional Prose', *Journal of English and Germanic Philology*, 76 (1977), 40–54.

41. See Knowles, *The English Mystical Tradition*, pp. 53 ff.; 84, 96, 107–9.

CHAPTER 2: IMAGINATION AND MYSTERY

1. Letter to Thomas Butts, 22 November 1802, ll. 87–8.

2. John of Ruysbroeck, *The Adornment of the Spiritual Marriage*, trans. C. A. Wynschenck (Westminster, Md.: Christian Classics, 1974), p. 156.

3. *Confessions*, VII, 23, trans. E. B. Pusey (London: J. M. Dent, 1907), pp. 138–9. Pusey glosses 'phantasms' with a quote from *De vera religione*, c. 10: '"Phantasms" are nothing else than figments drawn by the bodily senses from bodily forms; which, to commit to memory, as they have been received, to divide, multiply, contract, enlarge, order, disarrange, or in any other way image in the mind by thinking, is very easy; but to avoid and escape, where truth is sought, difficult' (p. 138).

4. *Dionysius the Areopagite on the Divine Names and the Mystical Theology*, trans. C. E. Rolt (London: Macmillan, 1920), pp. 197–8. Dionysius was probably a Syrian monk who lived at the end of the fifth century AD, and is sometimes known as pseudo-Dionysius because he was once held to be the Athenian convert of St Paul.

5. Charles Williams, *The Descent of the Dove* (Michigan: William B. Eerdmans, 1939), pp. 57–8.

6. Soren Kierkegaard, *The Sickness Unto Death*, trans. Walter Lowrie, *Fear and Trembling and the Sickness Unto Death* (New Jersey: Princeton University Press, 1941), p. 146. For the mirage and melancholy, see pp. 169 ff.

7. Augustine's contribution is crucial for the history of Western tradition: he is as Cuthbert Butler says, 'on all hands acknowledged to be the dominant figure in Western Christianity'. See *Western Mysticism* (London: Grey Arrow Books, 1960), p. 79. See also Robert J. O'Connell, *St. Augustine's Confessions. The Odyssey of Soul* (Cambridge, Mass.: Harvard University Press, 1969).

8. See Patrick Grant, *Images and Ideas in Literature of the English Renaissance* (London: Macmillan, 1979), pp. 3 ff.; Vernon T. Bourke, *Augustine's View of Reality* (Villanova, Pa.: Villanova University Press, 1964); Ronald H. Nash, *The Light of the Mind: St. Augustine's Theory of Knowledge* (Lexington: The University Press of Kentucky, 1969); Butler, *Western Mysticism*, p. 97, says of 'spiritual vision' that '"imaginary" is the best equivalent'.

9. John Freccero, 'Dante's Medusa: Allegory and Autobiography', in *By Things Seen: Reference and Recognition in Mediaeval Thought*, David L. Jeffrey (ed.) (Ottawa: Ottawa University Press, 1979), p. 33.

10. *I and Thou*, trans. Ronald Gregor Smith (New York: Charles Scribner's Sons, 1958), p. 3.

11. For further reading on such matters, see Illtyd Trethowan, *Mysticism and Theology. An Essay in Christian Metaphysics* (London: Geoffrey Chapman, 1975), pp. 4 ff., *et passim*; Owen Barfield, *History, Guilt and Habit* (Connecticut: Wesleyan University Press, 1979), pp. 67 ff.; James P. Mackey, *Jesus the Man and the Myth* (New York: Paulist Press, 1979), p. 137.

12. On children's verbal games and their social function, see Mary and Herbert Knapp, *One Potato, Two Potato. The Folklore of American Children* (New York: W. W. Norton, 1976).

13. *Phenomenology of Perception*, p. 6.

14. Sermon on Matthew 11:25, 26, in *Selected Sermons of St. Augustine*, Quincy Howe, Jr. (ed.) (New York: Holt, Rinehart and Winston, 1966), p. 224.

15. Recent research in mediaeval studies has helped to show that distinctions made by mediaeval philosophers and allegorists were often less a matter of frigid logic than what we might call an imaginative experience of the ideas. See C. S. Lewis, *The Discarded Image* (Cambridge: Cambridge University Press, 1964); A. D. Nuttall, *Two Concepts of Allegory* (London: Routledge and Kegan Paul, 1967); Paul Piehler, *The Visionary Landscape* (London: Edward Arnold, 1971).

16. On the quasi-theological task of Romanticism in context of traditional Christian thought, see M. H. Abrams, *Natural Supernaturalism. Tradition and Revolution in Romantic Literature* (New York: Norton, 1971).

17. *Prelude* (1850), II, 349–51.

18. 'The Harm that Good Men Do', in *Sceptical Essays* (London: George Allen and Unwin, 1928), pp. 112–13. Russell continues: 'Coleridge went through a similar change: when he was wicked he wrote Kubla Khan, and

when he was good he wrote theology'.

19. Bk. VI, Proem, st. 4: 'Amongst them all growes not a fayrer flowre/ Then is the bloosme of comely courtesie'.

20. See Maritain, *Creative Intuition in Art and Poetry*, pp. 234 ff.

21. 'The Song of the Happy Shepherd'.

22. *Imaginations and Reveries* (Dublin and London: Maunsel, 1915), p. 26.

23. *Essayes or Counsels*, XLVIII, 'Of Beauty', Richard Foster Jones (ed.) (New York: Odyssey Press, 1937), p. 125.

24. St Teresa, *Life*, Ch. 29, trans. E. Allison Peers (New York: Image Books), p. 275.

25. Blaise Pascal, *Pensées*, 913, Louis Lafuma (ed.) (Paris: Editions du Seuil, 1962), pp. 374–5. The fragment is known as Le Mémorial. See further, F. T. H. Fletcher, *Pascal and the Mystical Tradition* (Oxford: Basil Blackwell, 1954), esp. Ch. IV, 'The Mémorial', pp. 29 ff. Butler, *Western Mysticism*, pp. 74–5 takes a position similar to Underhill's with respect to the Mémorial.

26. Evelyn Underhill, *Mysticism* (New York: E. P. Dutton, 1961. First published, 1911), pp. 189–90.

27. David Jones, *The Dying Gaul and Other Writings* (London: Faber and Faber, 1978), p. 183

CHAPTER 3: HISTORICAL CRISES: FROM INCARNATION TO IMAGINATION

1. See Ernest Lee Tuveson, *Millennium and Utopia. A Study in the Background of the Idea of Progress* (New York: Harper Torchbooks, 1964); Thomas S. Kuhn, *The Structure of Scientific Revolutions*, 2nd edition, enlarged (Chicago: University of Chicago Press, 1970); Michael Polanyi, *Science, Faith and Society* (Chicago: University of Chicago Press, 1964. First published, 1946); *Knowing and Being*, Majorie Grene (ed.) (Chicago: University of Chicago Press, 1969), pp. 3 ff.; 73 ff.

2. Owen Barfield, *Romanticism Comes of Age* (Connecticut: Wesleyan University Press, 1966). p. 231.

3. See Jürgen Moltmann, *The Crucified God. The Cross of Christ as the Foundation and Criticism of Christian Theology*, trans. R. A. Wilson and John Bowden (London: SCM Press, 1974), p. 235.

4. *Mysticism*, p. 118.

5. *Sermons on the Canticle of Canticles*, XX, trans. by a priest of Mount Melleray, 2 vols. (Dublin: Browne and Nolan, 1920), I, 202. See further, Etienne Gilson, *The Mystical Theology of Saint Bernard*, trans. A. H. C. Downes (London: Sheed and Ward, 1940).

6. *The English Mystical Tradition*, p. 10.

7. *Western Asceticism*, Owen Chadwick (ed.), The Library of Christian Classics, vol. XII (Philadelphia: Westminster Press, 1958), pp. 51, 107. Christopher Dawson argues that the asceticism of the desert monks was not purely hostile to life; only by their going into the desert to make a fresh start could Christian ideals be raised to autonomy and independence. See *Enquiries into Religion and Culture* (New York: Sheed and Ward, 1934), p. 288.

8. See Claude Lévi-Strauss, *The Savage Mind* (Chicago: University of Chicago Press, 1966). 'The Logic of Totemic Classifications', pp. 40 ff.,

for a sense of the 'vast system of correspondences', at first strange and inaccessible to Western observers, yet comparable to Greek, Roman and Mediaeval emblem systems. See also Lucien Lévy-Bruhl, *How Natives Think*, trans. Lilian A. Clare (London: Allen and Unwin, 1926), pp. 352–8. Colin Turnbull's books, *The Mountain People* (New York: Simon and Schuster, 1972), and *The Forest People* (New York: Simon and Schuster, 1962), provide startling evidence of how social structure can affect mores.

9. See Ernesto Buonaiuti, 'Symbols and Rites in the Religious Life of Certain Monastic Orders', *The Mystic Vision: Eranos Yearbooks*, pp. 185 ff.; Ernst Robert Curtius, *European Literature and the Latin Middle Ages*, trans. Willard R. Trask (New Jersey: Princeton University Press, 1953), 'Mention of the Author's Name in Mediaeval Literature', p. 515.

10. See William J. Courtenay, 'Nominalism and Late Mediaeval Religion', in *The Pursuit of Holiness in Late Mediaeval and Renaissance Religion*, Charles Trinkaus, with Heiko A. Oberman (eds) (Leiden: E. J. Brill, 1974), pp. 26–59, for an assessment of past and present enquiries on the subject.

11. See Heiko A. Oberman, 'Some Notes on the Theology of Nominalism, with Attention to its Relation to the Renaissance', in *Harvard Theological Review*, LIII (1960), pp. 47–76.

12. For summaries, see Courtenay and Oberman, op. cit. and Paul Vignaux, *Philosophy in the Middle Ages. An Introduction*, trans. E. C. Hall (New York: Meridian Books, 1959).

13. The effect of nominalism on mysticism is, however, complex. See Steven Ozment, 'Mysticism, Nominalism and Dissent', in *Pursuit of Holiness*, pp. 67–92.

14. *The Cloud of Unknowing and Other Works*, trans. Clifton Wolters (Harmondsworth: Penguin Books, 1978), p. 51.

15. Gabriel Josipovici, *The World and the Book* (St Albans: Paladin Books, 1973), p. 61.

16. For an account of the contribution of St Teresa and St John of the Cross, see E. Allison Peers, *Studies of the Spanish Mystics* (London: SPCK, 1951), vol. I, Chapters IV and V, pp. 107–233. From this period, the distinction between acquired and infused contemplation becomes central to discussions of mysticism.

17. See especially Henri Brémond, *Histoire Littéraire du Sentiment Religieux en France* (Paris: Bloud et Gay, 1916–71). For an extended account of the following developments in France, see Patrick Grant, *Images and Ideas*.

18. For further reading in Bérulle, see Brémond, *Histoire Littéraire*, t. III, 'L'Ecole Francaise'; Paul Cochois, *Bérulle et L'Ecole Française* (Paris: Editions de Seuil, 1963); A. Molien, 'Bérulle', art., *Dictionnaire de Spiritualité Ascetique et Mystique Doctrine et Histoire*, Marcel Viller *et al.* (eds) (1937–), I, cols. 1539–81.

19. For further reading on Benet of Canfield, see Aldous Huxley, *Grey Eminence: A Study in Religion and Politics* (London: Chatto and Windus, 1944); Paul Renaudin, *Un maître de la mystique française: Benoit de Canfield* (Paris: 1956); Etta Gullick, 'The Life of Father Benet of Canfield', *Collectanea Franciscana*, vol. 42 (1972), pp. 39–67.

20. For further reading on Malebranche, see Pierre Blanchard, *L'Attention à Dieu Selon Malebranche* (Paris: Desclee De Brouwer, 1956); R. W. Church,

A Study in the Philosophy of Malebranche (London: 1931); Beatrice K. Rome, *The Philosophy of Malebranche. A Study of his Integration of Faith, Reason and Experimental Observation* (Chicago: Henry Regnery Co., 1963), Armand Cuvillier, *Essai sur la Mystique de Malebranche* (Paris: Librairie Philosophique, J. Vrin, 1954).

21. William Law is a notable exception: I discuss his mystical writings in the next chapter.

22. See Ernest Lee Tuveson, *The Imagination as a Means of Grace: Locke and the Aesthetics of Romanticism* (Berkeley: University of California Press, 1960).

23. *Natural Supernaturalism*, p. 89. See A. D. Nuttall, *A Common Sky. Philosophy and the Literary Imagination* (London: Chatto and Windus for Sussex University Press, 1974), p. 138: 'with all his great capacity for worship, he [Wordsworth] was always readier to reverence the proliferating effect than the First Cause'.

24. *Lehrbuch in Naturphilosophie* (1810), I, 26, trans. in Arthur O. Lovejoy, *The Great Chain of Being. A Study of the History of an Idea* (New York: Harper Torchbooks, 1960. First published, 1936), p. 321.

25. These are A. O. Lovejoy's terms: see *The Great Chain of Being*, esp. Chs IX and X, pp. 242 ff.

26. See *On Religion. Addresses in Response to its Cultured Critics*, V, trans. Terrence N. Tice (Richmond, Virginia: John Knox Press, 1969), pp. 272 ff.

27. Lovejoy, *The Great Chain of Being*, p. 313. See Auguste Saudreau, *The Life of Union with God*, trans. E. J. Strickland (London: Burns Oates and Washbourne, 1927), p. 312: 'The Nineteenth century did not give a single mystical author of the first rank to the Church'.

28. For further reading on Richard Jefferies, see W. J. Keith, *Richard Jefferies. A Critical Study* (Toronto: University of Toronto Press, 1965), which has a good bibliography.

29. Samuel J. Looker and Crichton Porteus, *Richard Jefferies, Man of the Fields. A Biography and Letters* (London: John Baker, 1964), p. 167. This book contains extensive excerpts from late, unpublished notebooks which add considerably to understanding of Jefferies' thought.

30. *The Story of My Heart* (London: Longmans, Green, 1907), pp. 146–7. Page numbers to this edition are cited hereafter in the text.

31. W. J. Keith, *Richard Jefferies*, p. 82.

32. Looker and Porteus, *Man of the Fields*, p. 166.

33. *The Origin of Species*, Ch. IV (New York: Collier, 1909), pp. 94–5.

34. See for instance, pp. 6, 9, 10, 11, 13, 15, 17, 18, 20, 25, 30, 45, 79, 85, 87, 106, 113, 114–16, 168, 182, 184, 199.

35. See Zaehner, *Mysticism, Sacred and Profane*, pp. 45 ff., and Keith, *Richard Jefferies*, pp. 84, ff.

36. Thus C. F. E. Spurgeon, *Mysticism in English Literature* (Cambridge: Cambridge University Press, 1913), pp. 70–1: 'it carries with it no vision and no philosophy. It is almost entirely emotional, and it is as an emotional record that it is of value, for Jefferies' intellectual reflections are, for the most part, curiously contradictory and unconvincing'.

37. Notebooks, in Looker and Porteus, *Man of the Fields*, p. 174.

38. Ibid., p. 169.

39. For the following collection of quotations, see William Robert Miller's anthology on the 'death-of-God' theme, *The New Christianity* (New York: Dell, 1967), pp. 299, 335, 349, 267.

CHAPTER 4: SELF AND EGO

1. 'Meditations in Time of Civil War'. See Rudolf Steiner, *Occult Science. An Outline*, trans. George and Mary Adams (London: Rudolf Steiner Press, 1979), p. 57: 'For what appears crudely material in the physical body is merely what is manifest in it'.

2. 'On the Psychology of the Unconscious', in *The Collected Works of C. G. Jung*, vol. VII, Herbert Read, Michael Fordham, Gerhard Adler (eds), trans. R. F. C. Hull (New Jersey: Princeton University Press, 1953), p. 175. See further, Louis Dupre, 'The Mystical Experience of the Self and its Philosophical Significance', *Proceedings of the American Catholic Philosophical Association*, 48 (1974), pp. 149–65.

3. 'Psychology and Alchemy', *Collected Works*, vol. XII (1953), p. 148.

4. See *Letters*, Gerhard Adler and Aniela Jaffé (eds), trans. R. F. C. Hull, 2 vols. (New Jersey: Princeton University Press, 1975), vol. II, pp. 52–3; 58 ff.; 71 ff.; 133 ff.; 163 ff.; 238 ff.

5. *Theologia Germanica*, trans. Susanna Winkworth (London: Longman, Brown, Green and Longmans, 1854), pp. 7 and 111.

6. *Adornment of the Spritual Marriage*, trans. Wynschenck, p. 25.

7. *A Treatise Against Eutyches and Nestorius*, III, trans. H. F. Stewart (Cambridge, Mass.: Harvard University Press, 1918), p. 85: 'naturae rationabilis individua substantia'.

8. It is advisable to distinguish the theological sense of person from the modern, psychological sense. See Karl Rahner, *The Trinity*, trans. Joseph Donceel (New York: Herder and Herder, 1970), pp. 103 ff.

9. *Epistle of Privy Counsel*, Ch. IV, in *The Cloud of Unknowing and other Treatises by an English Mystic of the Fourteenth Century*, with a commentary on the *Cloud* by Father Augustine Baker, OSB, Dom Justin McCann (ed.) (London: Burns Oates and Washbourne, 1924), p. 180; John of Ruysbroeck, *The Book of Supreme Truth*, Ch. IV, in *Adornment of the Spiritual Marriage*, trans. Wynschenck, p. 229.

10. See Jacques Maritain, *The Degrees of Knowledge*, trans. Bernard Wall and Margot Adamson (London: Centenary Press, 1937), pp. 382–3.

11. *Creative Intuition in Art and Poetry*, p. 143. See also pp. 120–1.

12. *The Anathemata* (London: Faber and Faber, 1952), Preface, p. 12.

13. *Descent of the Dove*, p. 195.

14. *A Serious Call to a Devout and Holy Life* (London: Everyman, 1906), pp. 137–8.

15. Ibid., p. 139.

16. James Boswell, *Life of Johnson*, G. Birbeck Hill (ed.) (Oxford: 1934), I, 68.

17. C. Walton, *Notes and Materials for an Adequate Biography of William Law* (1854), p. 26.

18. *Letters of C. S. Lewis*, W. H. Lewis (ed.) (London: Geoffrey Bles, 1966), p. 143.

19. For a summary account of Boehme's thought in relation to Law, see A. Keith Walker, *William Law. His Life and Thought* (London: SPCK, 1973),

Ch. 10, 'Jacob Boehme', pp. 96 ff.

20. *The Marriage of Heaven and Hell*, plate 3.

21. *The Spirit of Love*, in *The Works of the Reverend William Law* (London: J. Richardson, 1762), vol. VIII, p. 3. References hereafter are cited in the text.

22. *Letters of Aldous Huxley*, no. 485, To Alan Watts, 25 April 1944, Grover Smith (ed.) (London: Chatto and Windus, 1969), p. 504.

23. J. Byrom, *Private Journal and Literary Remains*, 2 vols. (Chetham Society, 1854–7), p. 204.

24. Letter of Thomas Lancake to Henry Brooke, 30 November 1782, cited in Desirée Hirst, *Hidden Riches. Traditional Symbolism from the Renaissance to Blake* (London: Eyre and Spottiswoode, 1964), p. 196.

25. Jean Pierre Camus, *The Spirit of St. Francis de Sales*, trans. J.S. (London: Burns and Oates, 1910), p. 214.

26. *Dark Night of the Soul*, II, 6, trans. E. Allison Peers, *The Complete Works of Saint John of the Cross*, II, 385–6.

CHAPTER 5: THE CROSS

1. *Of the Imitation of Christ*, II, 12, 4, trans. Abbot Justin McCann (New York: Mentor Books, 1957), p. 69.

2. See *Meister Eckhart*, Franz Pfeiffer (ed.), trans. C. de B. Evans (London: John M. Watkins, 1924), vol. I, pp. 262 ff.; 'Spiritual Sentences and Maxims', 13, in *Complete Works of Saint John of the Cross*, III, 228; Paul Tillich, *Dynamics of Faith* (New York: Harper and Row, 1958), pp. 97–8; Jürgen Moltmann, *The Crucified God*, p. 72.

3. See Henry C. Lea, *A History of the Inquisition of the Middle Ages*, 3 vols. (New York: Harper, 1900–1); E. Vacandard, *The Inquisition*, trans. Bertrand L. Conway (New York: Richwood Publishing Co., 1915).

4. *The Spirit of Love*, p. 82.

5. *The Mind's Road to God*, VII, 2–3, 5.

6. St Teresa of Avila, *Interior Castle*, trans. E. Allison Peers (New York: Image Books, 1961), pp. 229, 209.

7. *Analecta Hymnica Medii Aevi*, Guido M. Dreves, S.J., and Clemens Blume, S.J. (eds), 55 vols. (Leipzig: O. R. Reisland, 1886–1922), 8, 18, no. 11, st. 7, a–b.

8. See *De Civitate Dei*, XIX, 7; Ep. XLVII, 5; CXXXVIII, II, 13–14, cited in Herbert A. Deane, *The Political and Social Ideas of St. Augustine* (New York: Columbia University Press, 1963), pp. 154 ff.

9. Trans. John Gerard (Douay: 1603–10), A2 verso.

10. John of Ruysbroeck, *Adornment of the Spiritual Marriage*, Ch. XVIII, trans. Wynschenk, pp. 30–2.

11. See Moltmann, *The Crucified God*, pp. 303 ff.

12. A Protestant merchant of Toulouse, executed in 1762 proclaiming his innocence against a charge of murdering his son to prevent him from becoming a Catholic. Voltaire vindicated Calas, but not in time to save his life.

13. W. H. Auden, 'The Protestant Mystics', in *Forewords and Afterwords*, selected by Edward Mendelson (New York: Vintage Books, 1974), p. 52.

14. *The Butterfly Book* (New York: Doubleday, Page, 1920), pp. 299 ff.

15. Holy Sonnet XI, Helen Gardner (ed.), *John Donne. The Divine Poems*

(Oxford: Clarendon Press, 1964. First published, 1952), p. 9.
16. For the older 'Ignatian' view, see Louis Martz, *The Poetry of Meditation* (New Haven: Yale University Press, 1962); see also Barbara Lewalski, *Protestant Poetics and the Seventeenth-Century Religious Lyric* (New Jersey: Princeton University Press, 1979).
17. Simone Weil, *Waiting for God*, trans. Emma Craufurd (New York: Harper and Row, 1973. First published, 1951), pp. 123–4, 127, 135.

CHAPTER 6: THE WAY
1. For further reading see Stanley Fish, *Self-Consuming Artifacts. The Experience of Seventeenth-Century Literature* (Berkeley: University of California Press, 1972); C. S. Lewis, *Spenser's Images of Life*, Alister Fowler (ed.) (Cambridge: Cambridge University Press, 1967).
2. 'The Protestant Mystics', p. 51.
3. See *Life*, Ch. XIII, 24; Auguste Saudreau, *The Degrees of Spiritual Life*, 2 vols., trans. Dom Bede Camm (London: Burns, Oates and Washbourne, 1926), 'How Direction must be altogether Supernatural', I, 68 ff.
4. This brief historical synopsis is indebted to a number of sources. The following are especially recommended: Henri Brémond, *Histoire Littéraire*; Cuthbert Butler, *Western Mysticism*; Walter Holden Capps and Wendy M. Wright, *Silent Fire: An Invitation to Western Mysticism* (San Francisco: Harper and Row, 1978); William Fairweather, *Among the Mystics* (Edinburgh: T. and T. Clark, 1936); John Ferguson, *An Illustrated Encyclopaedia of Mysticism and the Mystery Religions* (London: Thames and Hudson, 1976); Anne J. Fremantle, *The Protestant Mystics* (Boston: Little, Brown, 1964); Hilda Graef, *The Story of Mysticism* (New York: Doubleday, 1965); Rufus Jones, *Studies in Mystical Religion* (London: Macmillan, 1909); several volumes in the Library of Christian Classics series, especially vol. I, *Early Christian Fathers*, Cyril C. Richardson (ed.) (Philadelphia: Westminster Press, 1953); vol. II, *Alexandrian Christianity*, Henry Chadwick and J. E. L. Oulton (eds) (1954); vol. XII, *Western Asceticism*, Owen Chadwick (ed.) (1958); *Late Mediaeval Mysticism*, Ray C. Petry (ed.) (1957); 'Mysticism', art., *Encyclopedia of Religion and Ethics*, James Hastings (ed.) (New York: Charles Scribner's Sons, 1910–34); 'Mysticism', art., *Sacramentum Mundi*; Pierre Pourrat, *Christian Spirituality in the Middle Ages*, trans. S. P. Jacques (Westminster, Md.: Newman Press, 1953); Karl Rahner, *Theological Investigations*, vol. III, *Theology of the Spiritual Life*, trans. Karl H. and Boniface Kruger (London: Darton, Longman and Todd, 1967), 'Reflections on the Problem of the Gradual Ascent to Christian Perfection', pp. 3 ff.; A. Ravier *et al.*, *La Mystique et les Mystiques* (Paris: Desclée de Brouwer, 1965); G. G. Scholem, *Major Trends in Jewish Mysticism* (New York: Schocken Books, 1961); Margaret Smith, *An Introduction to the History of Mysticism* (London: SPCK, 1930); E. Underhill, *The Mystics of the Church* (London: J. Clarke, 1925).
5. (a) I Cor. 3:1–2; Eph. 4:14; Heb. 5:12–13; (b) I Cor. 2:6, 14, 20; Ph. 3:15; (c) I Cor. 2:13, 15; 3:1; 14:37; Gal. 6:1.
6. Clement of Alexandria, *The Stomata, or Miscellanies*, VII, XIII, trans. A. Cleveland Coxe, *The Nicene Fathers*, vol. II (Buffalo: Christian Literature Publishing Co., 1885), p. 547.

7. Cuthbert Butler, *Western Mysticism*.
8. Henry David Thoreau, *Walden* (New York: Bantam Books, 1962), p. 253.
9. On rapprochment between East and West, see Owen Barfield, *Romanticism Comes of Age* (Connecticut: Wesleyan University Press, 1966); William Johnston, *The Still Point. Reflections on Zen and Christian Mysticism* (New York: Harper and Row, 1971); Hans Küng, *On Being a Christian*, trans. Edward Quinn (New York: Doubleday and Co., 1976), esp. Ch. III, 'The Challenge of the World Religions'; Thomas Merton, *Mystics and Zen Masters* (New York: Ferrar, Straus and Giroux, 1967); Rudolf Otto, *Mysticism East and West*, trans. Bertha L. Bracey and Richenda C. Payne (New York: Macmillan, 1932); Raimundo Panikkar, *The Unknown Christ of Hinduism* (London: Darton, Longman and Todd, 1964); *The Intrareligious Dialogue* (New York: Paulist Press, 1979). On the dangers of naive cultism, see Carroll Stoner and Jo Anne Parke, *All God's Children* (Harmondsworth: Penguin Books, 1979). Naivete threatens the learned too: Frits Staal, *Exploring Mysticism*, pp. 71, 104, points out the problems of grasping the content of many key words, such as those describing the effects of yogic exercises or stages of the kundalinī, which Western commentators sometimes incorrectly think they understand.
10. *Interior Castle*, trans. E. Allison Peers, p. 190. Further references are cited in the text.
11. See *Interior Castle*, 'Introduction', pp. 9 ff., for an account of P. Jerónimo Gracián's manuscript notes on how Teresa was persuaded to write the *Interior Castle*, and the pains taken by her, and her learned advisors, to assure correctness. See also Robert T. Petersson, *The Art of Ecstasy: Teresa, Bernini and Crashaw* (London: Routledge and Kegan Paul, 1970), pp. 14 ff.
12. Cuthbert Butler, *Western Mysticism*, 'Afterthoughts', pp. 9 ff.
13. Even Erasmus was regarded with disfavour in Spain, and was associated with Lutheranism and the supposedly false mysticism of the alumbrados. See Helmut A. Hatzfeld, *Santa Teresa de Avila* (New York: Twayne Publications, 1969), p. 13; John E. Longhurst, *Erasmus and the Spanish Inquisition: the Case of Juan de Valdés*, University of New Mexico Publications in History, no. 1 (Albuquerque: University of New Mexico Press, 1950); Marcel Bataillon, *Erasme et l'Espagne: Recherches sur l'histoire spirituelle du XVIe siècle* (Paris: 1937).
14. For an account of Teresa's prose style, see E. Allison Peers, *St. Teresa of Jesus, and Other Essays and Addresses* (London: Faber and Faber, 1953), pp. 81 ff., 'Saint Teresa's Style: A Tentative Appraisal'; Hatzfeld, *Santa Teresa*, pp. 23 ff.
15. *The Second Sex*, trans. H. M. Parshley (New York: Alexander Knopf, 1964), p. 714.

Bibliographical Guide
To Texts Without Comment

(I have often used distinguished older translations for the Texts Without Comment. More readily available modern editions are cited in the main body of the argument, with references in the footnotes.)

CHAPTER 1

1. St Bernard of Clairvaux, *St Bernard's Sermons on the Canticles*, 2 vols., trans. by a priest of Mount Melleray (Dublin: Browne and Nolan, 1920), I, pp. 467–8.

2. William of St Thierry, *The Golden Epistle of Abbot William of St Thierry to the Carthusians of Mont Dieu*, trans. W. Shewring, Dom Justin McCann (ed.) (London: Sheed and Ward, 1930), p. 20.

3. Thomas à Kempis, *Of the Imitation of Christ*, trans. C. Bigg (London: Methuen, 1905), p. 19.

4. St John of the Cross, *The Complete Works of Saint John of the Cross*, trans. David Lewis, the Oblate Fathers of Saint Charles (eds), Preface by Cardinal Wiseman, 2 vols. (London: Longman, Green, Longman, Roberts, and Green, 1864), II, pp. 182–3.

5. Richard Rolle, *The Fire of Love or the Melody of Love and the Mending of Life or Rule of Living*, trans. Richard Misyn, done into modern English by Frances M. M. Comper (ed.), intro. Evelyn Underhill (London: Methuen, 1914), p. 59.

6. Ibid., p. 65.

7. Meister Eckhart, *Meister Eckhart*, 2 vols., Franz Pfeiffer (ed.) (Leipzig: 1857), trans. C. de B. Evans (London: 1924), II, p. 7.

8. Benjamin Whichcote, *Select Notions* (London: 1685), p. 115.

9. John of Ruysbroeck, *The Adornment of the Spiritual Marriage; The Sparkling Stone; The Book of Supreme Truth*, trans. P. Wynschenk Dom (London: 1916). pp. 35–6.

10. John Tauler, *The Inner Way. Being Thirty-Six Sermons for Festivals by John Tauler*, trans. Arthur Wollaston Hutton (London: Methuen, 1901), pp. 97–8.

11. St Augustine of Hippo, *Expositions on the Book of Psalms*, vol. II, *A Library of the Fathers* (Oxford: John Henry Parker, 1848), XXV, p. 193.

12. Jacob Boehme, *The Works of Jacob Behmen, The Teutonic Theosopher*

(London: M. Richardson, 1764), I, p. 28.

13. Rulman Merswin, *Mystical Writings of Rulman Merswin*, trans. Thomas S. Kepler (Philadelphia: The Westminster Press, 1960), p. 130.

14. Angela of Foligno, *The Book of Divine Consolation of the Blessed Angela of Foligno*, trans. Mary G. Steegmann (London: New Mediaeval Library, 1908), p. 169.

15. St Bernard of Clairvaux, *Sermons on the Canticles*, I, p. 8.

16. William of St Thierry, *The Enigma of Faith*, trans. John D. Anderson (Washington, DC: Cistercian Publications, 1974), p. 37.

17. St Catherine of Siena, *The Dialogue of the Seraphic Virgin Catherine of Siena*, trans. Algar Thorold (London: Kegan Paul, Trench, Trübner, 1896), p. 64.

18. St Teresa of Avila, *The Interior Castle*, trans. the Benedictines of Stanbrook Abbey (London: 1912), p. 111.

19. William Law, *The Works of the Reverend William Law*, 9 vols. (London: 1782), VIII, p. 53

20. St Ignatius Loyola, *The Spiritual Exercises of St Ignatius of Loyola*, trans. W. H. Longridge (London and Oxford: A. R. Mowbray, 1919), p. 154.

21. Jean-Pierre de Caussade, *Abandonment to Divine Providence*, trans. E. J. Strickland (Exeter: The Catholic Records Press, 1925), p. 27.

22. Lorenzo Scupoli, *The Spiritual Conflict*, trans. John Gerard (Douay: 1603–10), Ch. 16.

23. Juan de Valdes, *The Hundred and Ten Considerations*, trans. N. Ferrar (Oxford: 1638), p. 99.

24. Thomas Merton, *New Seeds of Contemplation* (New York: New Directions, 1972; first published, 1962), pp. 134–5.

25. Jacob Boehme, *Works*, vol. II, part III, pp. 135–6.

26. St Augustine of Hippo, *A Select Library of the Nicene and Post-Nicene Fathers*, Philip Schaff (ed.) (New York: The Christian Literature Company, 1888), VII, p. 184.

27. Jean-Pierre de Caussade, *Abandonment to Divine Providence*, p. 17.

28. Origen, *The Ante-Nicene Fathers* (Buffalo: Christian Literature Publishing, 1885), IV, p. 400.

29. St Bernard, *Sermons on the Canticles*, I, p. 325.

30. St Gregory the Great, *The Dialogues*, trans. P. W. (Paris, 1608), Edmund G. Gardner (ed.) (London: Philip Lee Warner, 1911), p. 179.

31. Nicholas of Cusa, *The Vision of God*, trans. E. Gurney Salter (London: 1928), p. 43–4.

CHAPTER 2

1. Richard of St Victor, *Selected Writings on Contemplation*, trans. Clare Kirchberger (London: Faber and Faber, 1957), p. 254.

2. Julian of Norwich, *Revelations of Divine Love*, Grace Warwick (ed.) (London: Methuen, 1901), p. 26.

3. Ibid., p. 10.

4. Origen, *Selections from the Commentaries and Homilies of Origen*, trans. R. B. Tollington (London: SPCK, 1929), pp. 75–6.

5. Ibid., p. 40.

6. St Bonaventure, *The Works of Bonaventure*, vol. I, *Mystical Opuscula*, trans.

170   *Literature of Mysticism in Western Tradition*

José de Vinck (New Jersey: St Anthony Guild Press, 1960), p. 27.
7. Richard of St Victor, *Selected Writings*, pp. 91–2.
8. Meister Eckhart, *Meister Eckhart*, I, p. 186.
9. Benet of Canfield (William Fitch), *The Rule of Perfection* (Roan, 1609), p. 155.
10. Anonymous, *The Cloud of Unknowing and Other Treatises by an English Mystic of the Fourteenth Century*, with a commentary on the Cloud by Father Augustine Baker, OSB, Dom Justin McCann (ed.) (London: Burns, Oates and Washbourne, 1924), pp. 34–5.
11. Franciscus Ludovicus Blosius, *A Book of Spiritual Instruction*, trans. Bertrand A. Wilberforce (London and Leamington: Art and Book Co., 1900), p. 95.
12. Dionysius the Areopagite, *Dionysius the Areopagite on the Divine Names and the Mystical Theology* (London: SPCK, 1920), p. 191.
13. Simone Weil, *Waiting for God*, trans. Emma Craufurd (New York and London: Harper and Row, 1973), pp. 146–7.
14. Evagrius Ponticus, *Chapters on Prayer*, trans. John Eudes Bamberger (Massachusetts: Cistercian Publications, 1970), p. 79.
15. John Cassian, *A Select Library of the Nicene and Post-Nicene Fathers*, series II, (Oxford: 1894), XI, p. 303.
16. St Augustine of Hippo, *Nicene and Post-Nicene Fathers*, III, p. 127.
17. George Fox, *Book of Miracles*, ed. Henry J. Cadbury (Cambridge: At the University Press, 1948), p. 112.
18. Augustine Baker, *Sancta Sophia* (Douay: John Patte and Thomas Fievet, 1657), III, p. 14.
19. Meister Eckhart, *Meister Eckhart*, I, 186.
20. Madame Guyon, *A Method of Prayer*, trans. Dugald Macfadyen (London: James Clarke, 1902), pp. 64–5.
21. Miguel de Molinos, *The Spiritual Guide which Disentangles the Soul*, Kathleen Lyttleton (ed.) (London: Methuen, 1907), p. 116.
22. Evagrius Ponticus, *Chapters on Prayer*, p. 39.
23. Mechthild of Magdeburg, *The Revelations of Mechthild of Magdeburg* (1210–97), or, *The Flowing Light of the Godhead*, trans. Lucy Menzies (London: Longmans, Green, 1953), p. 108.
24. Benet of Canfield (William Fitch), *Rule of Perfection*, p. 152.
25. St Catherine of Genoa, *The Treatise on Purgatory*, trans. H. E. Manning (London: Burns and Lambert, 1858), p. 12.
26. John Tauler, *The Inner Way*, p. 3.
27. Thomas à Kempis, *Of the Imitation of Christ*, p. 84.
28. Fenelon, François de Selignac de la Mothe, *The Maxims of the Saints Explained* (London: H. Rhodes, 1698), p. 87.
29. Richard Jefferies, *The Story of My Heart* (London: Longmans, Green, 1907), p. 144.
30. St John of the Cross, *Works*, II, p. 379.
31. Ibid., II, p. 380.
32. John Tauler, *The Inner Way*, p. 205.
33. Anonymous, *The Cloud of Unknowing*, pp. 16–17.
34. John of Ruysbroeck, *Adornment*, etc., p. 241.
35. St Augustine of Hippo, *Confessions*, trans. E. B. Pusey (London:

Everyman, 1907), p. 260.
36. Thomas Traherne, *Centuries, Poems, and Thanksgivings*, H. M. Margoliouth (ed.), 2 vols. (Oxford: Clarendon Press, 1958), I, p. 143.
37. Meister Eckhart, *Meister Eckhart*, I, p. 180.

CHAPTER 3
1. Charles Williams, *Descent of the Dove. A Short History of the Holy Spirit in the Church* (London: The Religious Book Club, 1939), p1.
2. Nicholas of Cusa, *Vision of God*, p. 93.
3. John Tauler, *The Inner Way*, pp. 151–2.
4. Clement of Alexandria, *The Ante-Nicene Fathers* (Buffalo: The Christian Literature Publishing Co., 1885), II, p. 601.
5. Julian of Norwich, *Revelations*, pp. 153–4.
6. Simone Weil, *Waiting for God*, pp. 171–2.
7. St Bernard of Clairvaux, *Sermons on the Canticles*, II, p. 172.
8. Peter Sterry, *The Rise, Race and Royalty of the Kingdom of God in the Soul of Man, opened in several sermons upon Matthew 18:3 as also The Lovliness and Love of Christ set forth in several other Sermons upon Psal. 45.v.1, 2. Together with An Account of the State of a Saint's Soul and Body in Death* (London: Thomas Cockerill, 1683), p. 170.
9. Walter Hilton, *The Scale of Perfection*, modernised from the first printed ed. of Wynken de Worde, London, 1494, by an Oblate of Solesmes, with an Introduction by Dom M. Noetinger (London: Burns Oates and Washbourne, 1927), pp. 131–2.
10. Julian of Norwich, *Revelations*, p. 59.
11. William of St Thierry, *Enigma of Faith*, p. 46.
12. Miguel de Molinos, *The Spiritual Guide*, pp. 59–60.
13. Walter Hilton, *The Scale of Perfection*, p. 96.
14. Nicholas of Cusa, *The Vision of God*, pp. 26–7.
15. Meister Eckhart, *Meister Eckhart*, II, p. 53.
16. Richard of St Victor, *Selected Writings*, pp. 172–3.
17. St Gregory the Great, *Morals on the Book of Job*, trans. Rev. J. Bliss, **A** Library of the Fathers (Oxford: 1850), pp. 31, 403.
18. St Teresa of Avila, *Interior Castle*, p. 5.
19. William of St Thierry, *Golden Epistle*, p. 17.
20. Ibid., pp. 96–7.
21. St Ignatius Loyola, *Spiritual Exercises*, p. 200.
22. Anonymous, *Theologia Germanica*, trans. Susanna Winkworth (London: Longman, Brown, Green and Longmans, 1854), p. 183.
23. Mechthild of Magdeburg, *Revelations*, p. 41.
24. Jean-Pierre de Caussade, *Abandonment to Divine Providence*, pp. 57–8.
25. Thomas Traherne, *Centuries, Poems and Thanksgivings*, I, p. 189.
26. William Law, *Works*, VII, pp. 214–15.
27. Meister Eckhart, *Meister Eckhart*, I, p. 25.

CHAPTER 4
1. St John of the Cross, *Works*, I, pp. 224–5.
2. St Peter of Alcantara, *A Golden Treatise of Mental Prayer*, trans. George Seymour Hollings (London: A. R. Mowbray, 1905), p. 50.

3. St Augustine of Hippo, *Soliloquies*, A Select Library of the Nicene and Post-Nicene Fathers, VII, p. 547.
4. Anonymous, *Theologia Germanica*, pp. 110–11.
5. Ibid., pp. 173–4.
6. Benet of Canfield, *Rule of Perfection*, p. 88.
7. St François de Sales, *Letters to Persons in Religion*, in Library of St F. de Sales, trans. Dom H. B. Mackey (London: Burns and Oates, 1888), IV, p. 249.
8. Ibid., IV, p. 349.
9. St Bernard of Clairvaux, *Sermons on the Canticles*, I, p. 411.
10. St Benedict, *The Rule of the Holy Father Saint Benedict*, trans. N. N. (Douay: 1700), pp. 33–4.
11. John Cassian, *Conferences*, p. 388.
12. Walter Hilton, *The Scale of Perfection*, pp. 30–1.
13. Augustine Baker, *Sancta Sophia*, II, p. 424.
14. Juan de Valdes, *Considerations*, p. 209.
15. Meister Eckhart, *Meister Eckhart*, I, pp. 180–1.
16. Evagrius Ponticus, *Praktikos*, p. 24.
17. John Cassian, *Conferences*, p. 298.
18. Mechthild of Magdeburg, *Revelations*, p. 262.
19. St John of the Cross, *Works*, I, pp. 419–20.
20. Madame Guyon, *Spiritual Torrents*, trans. A. W. Marston (London: H. R. Allenson, 1908), p. 89–90.
21. George Fox, *A Journal or Historical Account of the Life, Travels, Sufferings, Christian Experiences, and Labour of Love in the Work of the Ministry of the Ancient, Eminent, and Faithful Servant of Jesus Christ*, 2 vols. (Leeds: Anthony Pickard, 1836), I, pp. 90–1.
22. Thomas Traherne, *Centuries, Poems, and Thanksgivings*, I, p. 118.
23. Lorenzo Scupoli, *The Spiritual Conflict*, p. 19.
24. Evelyn Underhill, *The Letters*, ed. Charles Williams (London: Longmans, Green, 1943), p. 308.
25. Evagrius Ponticus, *Chapters on Prayer*, p. 65.
26. John of Ruysbroeck, *Adornment*, etc., p. 32.
27. Thomas à Kempis, *Of the Imitation of Christ*, p. 108.
28. Anonymous, *Epistle of Privy Counsel*, in *The Cloud of Unknowing and Other Treatises*, p. 181.
29. John of Ruysbroeck, *Adornment*, etc., p. 229.
30. William Law, *Works*, IV, pp. 152–3.

CHAPTER 5
1. John Tauler, *The Inner Way*, p. 197.
2. St François de Sales, *A Treatise of the Love of God*, trans. Miles Car (Douay: Gerard Pinchon, 1630), p. 789.
3. St Augustine of Hippo, *Homilies on the Gospel of John*, Nicene and Post-Nicene Fathers, VII, p. 14.
4. Rulman Merswin, *Mystical Writings*, p. 59.
5. Evelyn Underhill, *Letters*, p. 105.
6. Henry Suso, *Little Book of Eternal Wisdom* (London: R. and T. Washbourne, 1910), p. 34.

7. Anonymous, *The Cloud of Unknowing*, p. 26.
8. Walter Hilton, *The Scale of Perfection*, p. 64.
9. Augustine Baker, *Sancta Sophia*, III, p. 125–6.
10. François Fenelon, *Maxims*, p. 107.
11. Ramon Lull, *The Book of the Lover and the Beloved*, trans. E. Allison Peers (London: SPCK, 1923), p. 51.
12. Ibid., p. 105.
13. St Bonaventure, *Works*, I, p. 58.
14. John of Ruysbroeck, *Adornment*, etc., pp. 98–9.
15. William of St Thierry, *Enigma of Faith*, pp. 63–4.
16. John of Ruysbroeck, *Adornment*, etc., p. 243.
17. Anonymous, *Dionise Hid Divinite*, in *The Cloud of Unknowing and Other Treatises*, p. 280.
18. Anonymous, *The Cloud of Unknowing*, pp. 80–1.
19. Evagrius Ponticus, *Chapters on Prayer*, p. 63.
20. Henry Suso, *Little Book*, p. 30.
21. St John of the Cross, *Works*, II, p. 346.
22. William Law, *Works*, IX, pp. 82–3.
23. Antoinette Bourignon, *A Collection of Letters written by Mrs Antonia Bourignon, Upon Occasion of the Many Persecutions rais'd against Her, for the Sake of the Truth* (London: 1708), p. 41.
24. Benjamin Whichcote, *Select Notions*, p. 86.
25. St John of the Cross, *Works*, II, p. 359.
26. William Law, *Works*, IV, p. 101.
27. Jacob Boehme, *Works*, I, pp. 97–8.
28. St Teresa of Avila, *Interior Castle*, p. 52.
29. St Catherine of Siena, *Dialogue*, p. 215.
30. John Cassian, *Conferences*, p. 419.

CHAPTER 6
1. Richard Rolle, *Fire of Love*, p. 88.
2. William of St Thierry, *Golden Epistle*, p. 26.
3. William Law, *Works*, IV, p. 85.
4. Meister Eckhart, *Meister Eckhart*, II, p. 60.
5. William of St Thierry, *Golden Epistle*, p. 23.
6. Ibid., p. 47.
7. Juan de Valdes, *Considerations*, p. 365.
8. St John of the Cross, *Works*, II, p. 366.
9. Augustine Baker, *Sancta Sophia*, I, p. 74.
10. Ibid., I, p. 75.
11. St Teresa of Avila, *Interior Castle*, pp. 207–8.
12. Jacob Boehme, *Works*, IV, pp. 98–9.
13. John of Ruysbroeck, *Adornment*, etc., p. 149.
14. John Tauler, *The Inner Way*, p. 104.
15. Clement of Alexandria, *Ante-Nicene Fathers*, II, p. 205.
16. Rulman Merswin, *Mystical Writings*, p. 122.
17. Ibid., p. 138.
18. Walter Hilton, *The Scale of Perfection*, pp. 229–30.
19. Richard of St Victor, *Selected Writings*, p. 247.

174   *Literature of Mysticism in Western Tradition*

20. Augustine Baker, *Sancta Sophia*, III, pp. 83–4.
21. Anonymous, *Theologia Germanica*, pp. 42–3.
22. St Gregory the Great, *Dialogues*, pp. 179–80.

Index

175